THE BACKYARD
blacksmith

THE BACKYARD
blacksmith

traditional techniques for the modern smith

LORELEI SIMS

BEVERLY MASSACHUSETTS

QUARRY BOOKS

First published in the United States
of America by
Quarry Books, a member of
Quayside Publishing Group
100 Cummings Center
Suite 406-L
Beverly, Massachusetts 01915-6101
Telephone: (978) 282-9590
Fax: (978) 283-2742
www.rockpub.com

**Library of Congress Cataloging-
in-Publication Data**

Sims, Lorelei.
    The backyard blacksmith : traditional
techniques for the modern smith /
Lorelei Sims.
        p.   cm.
    ISBN 1-59253-251-9 (pbk.)
    1. Blacksmithing—Amateurs' manuals.
I. Title.
    TT221.S56 2006
    682—dc22   2005034870
                                      CIP

ISBN-13: 978-1-59253-251-3
ISBN-10: 1-59253-251-9

14 13 12 11 10

Design: Dania Davey
Layout: Leslie Haimes
Photography: Daniel Broten
Illustrations: William Michael Wanke

Printed in Singapore

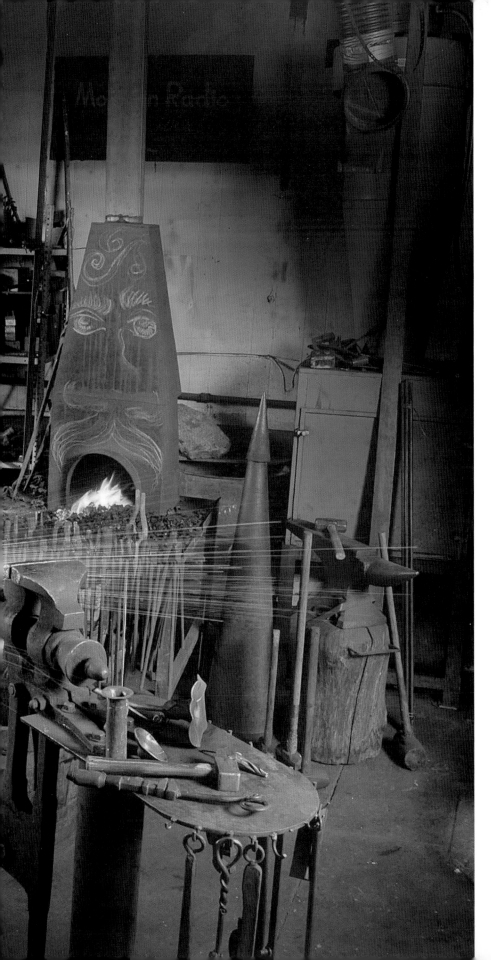

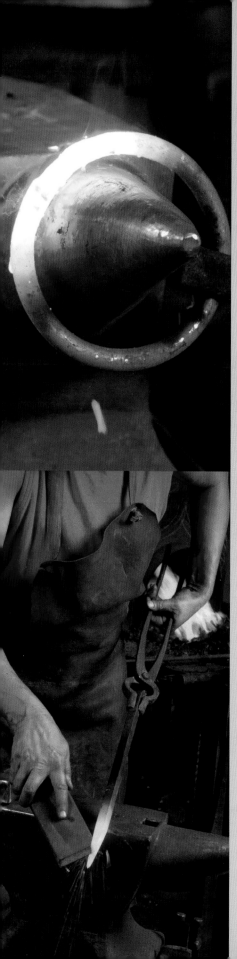

contents

Introduction

A touchmark is a blacksmith's way to sign their work.

My maternal great-grandfather, Soren Zachariassen, was a seventh generation coppersmith. At an early age, I was intrigued by his copperwork that filled my grandmother's home. Daily household items such as lamps, kettles, andirons, and vases, all fashioned by hand into beautiful and intricate forms, gave me an understanding that art could be functional. Inspired by his art, along with a series of events initiated with my undergraduate studies in art and sculpture, I pursued a path that led me to become an artist. In 1993, I opened Five Points Blacksmith Shop in Charleston, Illinois.

To achieve my vision, I incorporate traditional blacksmithing techniques and the use of modern equipment. My direct involvement in the transformation of metal, from raw material to finished product, gives me a spiritual connection to the process, as well as to the piece. Forging iron is a physically demanding process, but controlled movement is much more important than brute strength. Because I have been blacksmithing for more than a decade, repetitive motions such as tapering, flattening, scrolling, and texturing have actually become meditative. I am empowered by the creative possibilities that are available to me.

Forging iron is a physically demanding process, but controlled movement is much more important than brute strength.

My growth as an artisan is fueled by the knowledge that my work is enjoyed by many and that my business is valuable to my community.

Heat and hammer are the foundation of my craft, and the purpose of this book is to provide you with a practical understanding of the principal tools and techniques I use while working in my smithy. I am not a traditional blacksmith and though there may be several ways to perform a particular task, I will provide instruction that incorporates the methods I have found to be the most effective.

The successive introduction of blacksmithing techniques presented in this book will allow you to increase your skill level as you accumulate knowledge and experience. Once you are comfortable performing basic tasks, you will be able to create your own tooling—an invaluable resource for hobbyists and professional smiths. You will also be capable of completing a broad range of aesthetic and functional projects for your home and garden that will allow you to exercise a variety of blacksmithing skills.

As you enter the world of blacksmithing, this book and other resources will help you discover what best suits your interests as you continue to forge ahead. I feel very fortunate to make a living as a professional blacksmith and to be part of a great and ancient tradition that is no longer limited by gender-specific norms. My goal is to provide knowledge, insight, and inspiration to enthusiasts interested in implementing their own backyard smithy.

1 Getting Your Feet Wet

So you want to be a backyard blacksmith? The first thing we will do is review the essential information you need to know before lighting that forge. There is a lot of information available on the topic of blacksmithing. We are going to cover the basics.

CHAPTER ONE

YOUR SMITHY

Finding an appropriate location to set up your shop is a very significant endeavor that must be addressed. Although the next chapter discusses the basic tools and equipment you will use, first you need to figure out where you can establish your space. No matter the location, there are practical safety issues that must be considered when setting up and working in your smithy.

My smithy in Charleston, Illinois.

Selecting a Site

The location where a blacksmith works is called a smithy. There are a variety of spaces that can be used as your smithy: a garage, a barn or metal storage shed, or you may opt for a structure not located at your home. The most important aspects to consider when selecting a site are adequate light and ventilation, a weather-proof structure, and because of the noise created by hammering and the smoke created by burning coal, your smithy's proximity to surrounding neighbors. Many communities have zoning and noise regulations, and you need to determine if a permit is required for your blacksmithing activities. My shop is located in a mixed-zoning area, with houses and apartments as well as commercial space. I do my best to limit noisy activities to the hours between 8 AM and 5 PM.

—⁓—

One of my favorite past times is to listen to black-smiths talk about their first shops. I've heard of every-thing from a smith working in an old chicken coop to a smith working under a makeshift lean-to hidden under the trees in a backyard. I have seen mobile smithies wheeled out of a shed and set up under a tarped roof. Everyday, at the close of work, the tools and equipment are returned to the shed. If the blacksmith bug has bit-ten you, you don't care about where you are forging as much as you care about when you are forging!

—⁓—

It is imperative that your smithy has high ceilings, good lighting, and proper air ventilation. Once you have a structure in mind, you need to make sure that you have an adequate electrical source. Although tra-ditional blacksmithing tools and equipment do not require electricity, you need good lighting for your shop. If you intend on using an electric blower for your forge, make sure to ground the wiring; remember that you are surrounded by metal equipment and materials—all excellent conductors of electricity.

It is important for most of your shop to be well illuminated, but the actual area of the forge and anvil should be the darkest part of your smithy; too much light, whether it is natural or electric, makes viewing the color temperatures of heated metal more difficult to detect.

The air quality in a blacksmith shop can be some-what compromised; coal fire fumes and dust will loom in the air. Ventilation is mandatory for any enclosed space. Your coal forge will need a chimney that directs smoke outside. If you decide to work outside under a tarp or beneath a lean-to, the need for a chimney is no longer necessary.

It is important to maintain ventilation in your workspace, and many smiths keep their shop windows and doors open to help circulate fresh air into the smithy. My shop is located in an old service station garage so I am fortunate to have overhead bay doors located across from each other in my building. This works great during mild weather, but it's a whole dif-ferent story during the winter.

Setting Up Your Work Space

The layout of equipment is much more important than the square footage of your shop. Your tools and equip-ment should be set up efficiently. The three primary pieces of equipment in your shop—the forge, anvil, and post vise—should be positioned in a triangular pattern. The goal is to have the equipment situated so that you will be taking the shortest amount of steps between them, but with enough space around each piece of equipment to use it effectively.

It is ideal to have the forge located close to a wall. This will free up some open floor space and you will have access to position longer stock materials into the hearth from the three open sides. It is essential for your health and well being that the forge is set up properly, with an operational chimney and hood that

CONCRETE VERSUS DIRT FLOORING

There is a debate among practicing blacksmiths over what is the best flooring choice for your smithy. All blacksmiths agree that it is unsafe to work on flammable surfaces such as wood or linoleum. The two primary floor types found in a smithy are either dirt or concrete. Each material has attractive characteristics and your choice will be determined by your personal preference (or it may already be predetermined if you have an appropriate, ready-made site).

My shop floor is made of concrete. Concrete is an excellent drawing canvas. I use chalk to make scaled drawings on my floor, and when I am forging out sections of a project, I use the drawing as a guide to make sure that my pieces are appropriately shaped. If your concrete floor is level, it can be used as a surface to assemble your projects. Concrete is easy to maintain; I use a broom and air compressor hose to collect and dispose of debris. This type of flooring material also provides a good foundation to mount stationary equipment. Concrete can be poured in just about any location. The downside is that it's hard on your feet and legs to stand on concrete all day. If you have a concrete floor, place heavy rubber industrial mats in your work areas, excluding the forge and anvil space. This helps to soften your standing surface.

My solution to working on a concrete floor resides in my footwear—I spend money on the best boots available. I also insert arch supports and wear comfortable, thick, cotton work socks.

Blacksmiths rarely stand in one place without movement. We are active throughout the day and modern smiths move to and from different work stations other than the anvil and forge (for welding, plasma cutting, grinding, etc.).

Dirt floors have a nostalgic quality, are very cheap to install, and are attractive because they absorb noise within your shop and provide a softer surface for you to stand upon when working in your smithy. Over time, a dirt floor becomes just as solid as concrete, with little dirt and dust laying on the surface.

In preparing a dirt floor for a blacksmith shop, compact the ground by sprinkling water over the dirt, packing it down, and letting it dry. Repeat this process for several weeks until the surface area where your forge and anvil will sit is hard and level.

A natural material alternative to dirt is pea gravel. If your location has a dirt floor, use a water hose to make mud and pour a layer of pea gravel onto the mud. In order to embed the gravel into the dirt, alternately use a gardener's tamp and your water hose until there are no loose pieces. Pea gravel is not dusty, but this floor material is still not as easy to keep clean as concrete.

If you already have an existing space available, it is best to work with what's there, but shops that are built from scratch can incorporate several different floor surfaces. Pea gravel can be used at the forge and anvil with concrete poured for the rest of the work area.

adequately draws the coal smoke out of your shop. The chimney flue needs to extend at least three feet above the roof line.

Once the forge is in place, the anvil should go within 3 feet (0.9 m), or a stride, of it. This allows you to easily remove hot metal from the forge and bring it to the anvil. Position the anvil on the same side as the blower on the forge; this will give you immediate access to the anvil, forge, and forge blower in the same area.

Water is used to control the coal forge fire as well as to quench and cool hot metal. Your quench bucket should be placed as close to the forge as possible. I use a half-barrel from a garden center and have it located in front of the forge.

Every blacksmith shop should be equipped with a work bench and storage racks. A work bench will provide you with a staging area for your projects. Storage racks can be used to house your metal stock as well as to organize and store the tools you will be collecting and making. Organize your workshop so that everything has a designated place; make sure that items are secure and are not protruding into open spaces. A messy shop is an accident waiting to happen—my shop has been characterized as "organized chaos." Although it may appear cluttered to an outsider eye, everything has its place, and it is organized so that I can find everything easily and efficiently.

FORGING AREA LAYOUT

Here is a diagram which shows the layout of the forging area in my shop. Notice that the equipment follows a basic triangle pattern.

Trick of the Trade

The anvil should be positioned so that the horn is not protruding into the area between the forge and the anvil. Trust me, it really hurts to have an anvil horn jabbed into your thigh, and it's not something you need to experience for yourself.

Safety Equipment

There are several mandatory items listed here that should be accessible within your shop at all times.

—ɷ—

The one question that I am always asked whenever I demonstrate blacksmithing is whether or not I have ever gotten burned. The answer is, "yes, but I'm over him."

—ɷ—

FIRST AID KIT

Besides the basics—hydrogen peroxide, gauze bandages, eye wash, needle, tweezers, iodine, and so on, make sure that your first aid kit contains appropriate burn remedies, such as aloe vera and triple antibiotic lotion—essential when working with hot metal.

HOSE

Attach a garden hose and nozzle to either an indoor or outdoor spigot; although you do not want it stored in your immediate forging area, locate it where it will be available on short notice. If you do not have access to a continual water source, always have several buckets of water available in addition to a full quench bucket.

FIRE EXTINGUISHER

While water is enough to control a small forge fire, every shop should have at least one fire extinguisher; oil and other flammable liquids cannot be contained with water. Most extinguishers are regulated to varying performance standards. I have several small ones mounted in different locations throughout my shop. It is important to comply with insurance company standards that require clear signage indicating the extinguishers' locations—anyone would be able to quickly find one in my shop if an emergency arose.

Safety Tip

For minor burns, including second-degree blister burns no more than 2 to 3 inches (5 to 8 cm) in diameter, cool the burn under cold running water. This is important because even after the initial burn, skin continues to "cook."

By keeping the burned area under cold water for several minutes, you will decrease the temperature of the skin, which isolates the trauma and numbs the nerves. Apply an aloe vera lotion or a triple antibiotic ointment, cover the burn with a sterile gauze bandage, and take an over-the-counter pain reliever.

Do not apply ice directly to the burn; it may cause frostbite which will further damage the skin tissue. Do not break a blister—it protects the wound against infection. If a blister breaks, wash the area with mild soap and water, apply triple antibiotic ointment, and wrap it with a bandage.

Signs of infection include increased pain, redness, fever, swelling, and seepage. If an infection develops, seek medical attention.

General Safety Considerations

Never plan to work in your smithy if you are tired. In order to work safely and efficiently, you need to remain focused and organized. This is especially important if you will be working alone. Use your head and be proactive, not reactive. Be aware of the dangers of metalworking and have a plan should something go wrong.

I am not the only blacksmith who has admitted that part of their attraction to this ancient craft is the element of danger. Fire is our friend and we have all been reminded not to treat the relationship haphazardly. When knowledge, discipline, respect, and awareness come together, a natural feeling of empowerment is created. Blacksmithing is a noble craft that forges each smith's personal character.

It is virtually impossible to maintain a safe working environment if tools, stock, and debris are scattered around the floor. Keep your smithy clean and organized by following this advice.

SHOP ETIQUETTE

- Do not allow others inside your working triangle —vise, anvil, and fire—when you are forging. Visitors should stay on the far side of the anvil.

- All visitors should dress appropriately and wear safety glasses.

- Make sure that your workshop is well lit and properly vented.

- Store all flammable liquids outside of your immediate shop area.

- Remember that this is for enjoyment; take a break when you feel rushed or frustrated.

TOOLS

- Use hand tools only for their intended purpose.

- Before using a hammer, check the head to make sure it is tight on the hammer handle.

- Never use **tongs** that do not fit your metal stock and never hammer on metal stock that is not tightly held. Always assume that tong **jaws** are hot, and grab tongs by the handles only.

- Do not lean on the vise or rest your hand on the vise—always assume that the jaws are hot and that you could get pinched by the vise jaws. When not using your vise, close the jaws and if you have a post vise, rotate the handle into a vertical position when not in use—one less thing for you to run into.

- Anvil tools, especially the hot and **cold cut** hardies, should be removed from the **hardy hole** immediately after use.

- Always cool off tools by letting them air dry before putting them away.

- Check all edged tools for sharpness before use.

- If you have power tools in your shop, never remove any of the safety shields.

MATERIALS

- Do not heat any metal that is enclosed, such as a cast ball or a close-ended pipe—air expands when heated and the object could explode in your forge.

- Never heat galvanized metal or metal with a bright finish in your forge. The fumes from the coatings are very toxic.

- If you are unsure of the temperature of a piece of metal, pass your hand over it before picking it up.

- If there are visitors or other workers in your shop, announce loudly and clearly when you are walking around with hot metal stock.

- Always keep hot metal on the floor, near your immediate work area, but not within the equipment triangle.

Protection and Clothing

Hopefully you have accepted the fact that minor burns, cuts, and scrapes are inevitable when working with cold or hot metals. However, by following these guidelines, you should reduce the risk of injury.

CLOTHES

Always wear clothing made of cotton, wool, or other natural fibers when working at your forge. Natural materials are comfortable because they breath and absorb moisture. Although natural fibers burn and scorch, they do not smolder like synthetics. Synthetic materials are flammable and when exposed to heat, they will melt, adhere to the skin, and cause very bad burns.

Your attire should be close fitting at the neck and sleeves with no upturned cuffs. You shouldn't wear loose shirt tails, or torn or loose clothing. Dress in pants long enough to cover the top of your shoes. Many smiths wear a leather apron; this provides additional protection against sparks and hot flying metal.

Keep your hair pulled back and away from your face. You can cover your hair with a bandanna, baseball cap, or a welder's cap which features a built-in cotton sweatband. It is also recommended to remove any jewelry.

BOOTS

Steel-toed leather boots are ideal for blacksmithing but other leather boots or hi-top leather sneakers are suitable as well. Avoid any type of low-cut shoe or synthetic material. Hot sparks and slag can easily fall into low-cut shoes, and synthetic materials will melt. Hard rubber soles will smoke if you stand on a hot piece of metal; the smell of burning rubber will alert you before the hot metal burns through.

SAFETY GLASSES

Do not skimp on safety glasses. They should be mandatory for all visitors in your workspace. Proper safety glasses should have impact-resistant lenses with good side shields, and they should be worn in your shop at all times. It is important that your safety glasses fit well; otherwise you will be

Protective clothing and safety gear should always be worn when working in your shop.

constantly repositioning them when you are sweating. I prefer safety glasses that have a rubber nose bridge because the bridge provides a cushion and helps the glasses stay in place.

The most important function of safety glasses is to prevent fire scale from getting in your eyes. Fire scale is the oxidation that occurs when metal is heated; any time that hot metal is impacted, there exists the potential for fire scale to flake off. Fire scale is warm and can singe any part of your body, especially eye tissue.

If you happen to use an electric grinder while dressing a tool or while working on a project, plastic goggles will provide additional protection. Sparks have a way of navigating around regular safety glasses and finding your eyeball. Goggles seal off and protect the entire area.

GLOVES

Although there are numerous activities within a smithy that are best done while wearing gloves, forging is not one of them. Some smiths wear no gloves, while others leave their hammer hand bare and wear a glove on the other. It is very difficult to firmly grip a hammer while wearing a glove, but it can be learned and done. If you choose to wear a glove on your hammer hand, buy the thinnest suede or buckskin leather glove available.

Always wear a glove when you are wire brushing or filing hot metal as the slag flies randomly through the air, and your hand is the closest landing surface.

—⚒—

Because I am right handed, I go through a slew of left-handed gloves and am left with a box of virtually unused right gloves. I need to find a left-handed blacksmith to trade my gloves with.

—⚒—

A forging glove should be loose enough so that it can be shaken off without any assistance. Tight gloves are difficult to remove, especially when damp from sweat. Once you begin to feel searing heat through the glove material, it is almost too late to avoid getting burned.

Cotton gloves do not provide adequate protection because they catch fire easily and offer virtually no barrier between your skin and hot metal. As suggested with clothing, do not wear synthetic materials because they will melt when exposed to heat. One exception is Kevlar gloves—the material is engineered for working with hot metal and they do not burn or react much with fire. Leather gloves provide all-purpose protection. They can be used at the forge as well as during other smithing activities.

EAR PROTECTION

Blacksmith shop noise levels vary greatly, and it is not uncommon for older smiths to have hearing loss. The ringing of an anvil usually exceeds 85 decibels and it is important for you to take protective measures.

There are several different styles of ear protection available. The muff or cup style covers the entire ear, and the plug style goes directly into the outer ear canal. I prefer the little yellow rubber cone plugs attached to a blue plastic ring. These allow for me to converse without having to remove them, and the design allows for them to hang securely around your neck when not in use.

Avoid using disposable foam plugs that are sold as pairs in sealed packets. They do not work as well as other types of protection and every time you insert them in your ears, you have to roll the plugs between your fingers, which transfers dirt into your ears.

Your smithy reflects your personality. If you plan to consider blacksmithing commercially, the location of your studio is very important. If you are more inclined toward being a hobbyist, you may want to opt for co-sharing the expenses of a studio with another person. There are benefits to co-opting space, but it is completely understandable if you prefer to have your own space. There are many options available if you make an effort to explore the possibilities.

CHAPTER TWO

GATHERING TOOLS
AND EQUIPMENT

There are certain tools and equipment necessary for a functional workspace. This chapter provides information on the tools and equipment you will need to set up your smithy and includes suggestions on additional tools that will help you as you expand on your metalworking efforts.

It is important to note that all of this equipment can be purchased new or used, and in some cases, you can make your own. The resource section of this book includes reputable suppliers to help you determine what products will best suit your needs. I highly recommend buying second-hand equipment as a means of gathering tools and supplies. The majority of the equipment I use on a daily basis has been collected from auctions, garage sales, conference tailgate sales, and junkyards. I enjoy my shop's mixed-breed status of tools and equipment. The older pieces have their own histories that provide a sense of authenticity and old world charm, while new technology allows me to operate my smithy in today's fast-paced world.

ANATOMY OF AN ANVIL

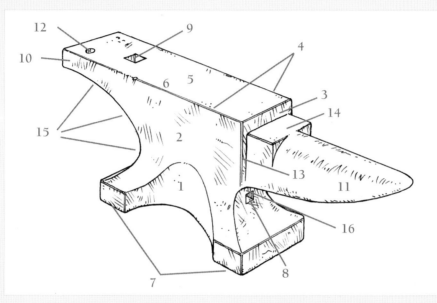

1. **Base**—All parts of an anvil from the waist downward.
2. **Body**—The area of the anvil from the waist up, including the face, heel, and horn.
3. **Drop**—The space from the face to the table.
4. **Edge**—The perimeter of the face.
5. **Face**—The main part of the anvil that is parallel to the floor. Most of your forging work will be performed on this area of the anvil.
6. **Face Plate**—A hardened steel plate welded to the face of the anvil. Usually $1/4$" to $3/4$" (0.5 to 2 cm) thick.
7. **Feet or Legs**—The four corners of the base that project outward.
8. **Handling Holes**—Rounded or square holes located in the waist or feet of the anvil.
9. **Hardy or Hardie Hole**—A squared shaped hole located on the tail of the anvil; used to secure anvil tools such as swages and chisels.
10. **Heel or Tail**—An overhanging projection that extends from the face of the anvil, opposite from the horn. The top of the heel is part of the face, and it provides a location for the hardy and/or pritchel holes.
11. **Horn or Beak**—A fairly soft and somewhat cone-shaped projection that extends near the table.
12. **Pritchel Hole**—A round-shaped hole located on the tail of the anvil; used primarily for punch work.
13. **Shoulder**—Area above the waist and below the face.
14. **Table or Chipping Block**—The rectangular surface located between the horn and the face of the anvil, usually stepped down from the face.
15. **Throat**—The areas between the horn and feet and the heel and feet.
16. **Waist**—The area located between the body and the base.

Anvil

The anvil is a block of iron on which hot metal is formed by hand and hammer. Anvils are available in a wide assortment of shapes and sizes—anywhere from a small jeweler's version that can be held in your hand, to a 600 pound (272 kg) or heavier behemoth.

The first commercially manufactured anvils were solid cast iron, and later, cast iron with a face plate—a separate piece of hardened steel forge-welded to the face. Around the turn of the twentieth century, cast steel anvils made from tool steel were introduced into the marketplace, and they are the predominant type of anvil manufactured today. Another option available is a forged steel anvil. German-made Peddinghaus anvils have a forged base with a forged-tool steel body and a hardened steel face. There are many new quality anvils on the market today.

The most important considerations when selecting an anvil for your smithy are size and general condition. The age of an anvil is irrelevant; older styles have different shapes and proportions but perform the same basic functions. I recommend an anvil somewhere in the 150 to 200 pound (68 to 90 kg) range. Anything smaller may not provide you with enough stability or an adequate working surface when forging your steel.

Remember, you can make small pieces on a large anvil, but it is harder to make large pieces on a small anvil. Also, the larger anvils have enough surface area to accommodate a secondary smith or striker. A striker is another blacksmith who swings a sledge hammer during some forging processes. Although it is unlikely that you will be starting out with a striker, there's nothing wrong with planning for the future. Remember that almost any kind of anvil can be used for your metalwork, and the most influential factors affecting price are whether the anvil is new or used, the manufacturer's reputation, and its overall condition.

It is normal for a used anvil to have a worn face, but it should be relatively free of chips and large indentations. The overall appearance of the anvil should be intact without any large chunks broken off.

2 + 2 DOES NOT ALWAYS EQUAL 4

The size of an anvil is given in weight, which is traditionally marked on the anvil's base or side. Older British anvils are marked using a numbering system based on the British hundredweight measuring system. Newer and American-made anvils have their actual weight marked in pounds or kilograms.

In the British weight system, there are 20 hundredweights in a ton, and a ton is equivalent to 2,240 American pounds. Therefore, one British hundredweight is equal to 112 American pounds.

These old-style anvils have three numbers stamped on their side. The first number represents hundredweight, the second number represents pounds as quarters of a hundredweight, and the third number represents an actual weight in simple pounds.

So, using this formula, an anvil marked 2-2-7 does not mean that it weighs 227 pounds. Its weight is calculated in the following manner:

2 = 112 pounds x 2 = 224 pounds

2 = $^2/_4$ or half of 112 pounds = 56 pounds

7 = 7 pounds = 7 pounds 227 anvil weighs = 287 American pounds

It is okay if the step of the anvil is marred because its specific purpose is to provide an area for chisel and cutting work.

When purchasing a used anvil, inspect the three most commonly used work surfaces for excessive pitting, chips, cracks, or separation.

• **Face**—Avoid an anvil whose face has excessive depressions. Dips are really difficult to fix, so look for an anvil face that is flat and even. If the face plate is cracked or seems to be separating from the body it will be expensive to repair.

The "ring" of the anvil is the best indicator of the face plate's condition. Use a hammer to lightly tap the face. A dull or muffled sound indicates that the hardened face plate has begun to separate from the body. A solid anvil has a ring like a bell.

• **Edges**—Normal wear on a used anvil results in chipped edges. If the chips are small in size, the affected area can usually be repaired with a modern specialty welding rod and a grinder.

• **Horn**—Check the horn for flat sides or excessive marring. Usually a grinder can be used to redress the horn.

Anvil Stand

Any movement of the anvil during the forging process dilutes the force of your hammer blows and will cause frustration, miscalculation, and possibly an accident. Therefore, your anvil is only as good as your stand.

The most traditional stand used is a large tree stump made of elm, oak, or another type of non-splitting wood. The anvil can be attached to the stump with spikes driven through the handling holes, spikes driven into the wood and bent over the anvil legs, or spikes driven through holes in metal straps which are secured over the anvil's feet.

Because it is very important that the top and bottom of the stump be level, it may be difficult to find a suitable tree stump. Most smiths opt for making their own anvil stands. I have seen stands fashioned from layered wood planks, sturdy wood boxes filled with sand, angled-iron floor mounts, and fabricated steel plate stands with truncated pyramid bases.

Buying a new anvil also means doing some clean up work as well. Most new anvils have sharp edges that need to be rounded up or dressed.

Give your new anvil's outer edge a slight radius near the step and horn to help in **scrolling** procedures. I use a grinder with a flap disc. It is aggressive but leaves a very smooth surface.

Keep the outer edge near the heel sharp. This area is used to make sharp, angled bends. Some blacksmiths use this sharp edge as a cutting edge, but I highly recommend against doing this. Your anvil should not be used as a cutting tool while learning to blacksmith—doing so will result in unnecessary damage to the anvil and your hammer.

The horn will need to be dressed as well. Use a grinder to shape the radius and **taper** of the horn, but do not bring it to a point. A horn tip radius that is too wide at the tip will impede some scrolling operations, and a horn tip that is too sharp can be somewhat dangerous to work around.

ANVIL STAND DESIGN

My anvil stand design was taken from Elmer Roush's shop in Brasstown, North Carolina, where I served as an apprentice. It is constructed from 3/16 inch (4.5 mm) plate steel welded into a four-sided tapered box that is filled with sand. The top plate of the stand is slightly larger than the stand base of my anvil—it is a separate piece of metal that is not attached to the base that rests or floats on top of the sand.

This design has several advantages over other commonly used stands:

1. The height is adjustable. If I am using a striker (secondary smith), I can lower the height of the top floater plate by removing sand from the base, thus lowering the anvil's height.

2. The stand is portable. The weight of the sand anchors my anvil stand securely enough that I get the same leverage as a stand that is floor-mounted. I can relocate the anvil station by simply removing and refilling the sand once I have moved the stand.

3. The stand absorbs sound and impact. The sand absorbs some of the ringing that occurs when forging. This is important to me because even though it is very nostalgic to hear the anvil "sing"—its ringing, all day long, everyday, is a bit overbearing.

Instructions for fabricating a metal anvil stand are included in Chapter Seven.

Two different anvils on two different stands: a double **bick** anvil on a sand-filled metal stand (left) and a farrier's anvil on a log stand. Notice that both stands have racks that house hardy tools.

Trick of the Trade
To help combat the ever present "PING, PING, PING" sound, I attach a large magnet under the heel of the anvil. This absorbs higher pitch noises but does not affect the anvil's ability to lift the hammer after each blow.

Whatever type of stand you choose, remember that its purpose is to secure the anvil at a proper working height. It is also very convenient if your stand features storage racks for hand and hardy tools. If you use a stump for your anvil stand, you can drive in brackets on the perimeter edge to hold your tooling.

Before selecting or making an anvil stand, you must determine the proper height of the anvil face. The best way to get the correct height measurement is to stand with your hammer arm hanging straight down by your side. Grasp a hammer or make a fist and have someone measure the distance between the floor and your knuckles.

The height of the anvil face should be just below your knuckles.

Once an anvil is set up, and you are standing next to it with your arms relaxed and hanging by your sides, the height of the anvil face should be just below your knuckles. Proper height allows the blacksmith to use full hammer blows and enables him to work comfortably without having to bend over. If the anvil is too high, your neck, shoulders, and elbows will sound the alarm. If the anvil is too low, your lower back will feel the strain.

Hammer

When starting out, you need only a few hammers for forging, texturing, and other hammering operations. As your skills increase, you will be able to add additional hammer styles and weights that are best suited for your increasing strength.

A general rule is to start out with the 1½ to 3 pound (0.7 to 1.4 kg) range for your hot metal forging hammers and something in the 3 to 5 pound (1.4 to 2.3 kg) range for your handheld sledge.

Hammers are characterized by the shape of their head and their weight. The head of a hammer is constructed of hardened tool steel and it has two sides—the face and the peen. The face is the largest work surface of the tool. It can be either square or round, and the surface is either completely flat or may have a slight, rounded convex surface. The peen is the opposite of the face, and there are many different styles of peens. The opening where the handle is inserted is called the eye. The eye of the hammer is oval shaped and slightly tapered, with the handle inserted into the larger opening.

Safety Tip

If the hammer is too light, you could get Carpenter's Elbow, a pinched feeling in the elbow and the top of your forearm where the elbow bends. An undersized hammer promotes the tendency to push down your arm in order to create a forced impact with the materials, undermining the objective of allowing the hammer weight and gravity to do the work for you.

If the hammer is too heavy for your arm muscles, you will feel it in your elbow, but also in the shoulders and wrist. In time you will increase your strength and efficiency, and you will need to have a few different sizes of your favorite style forging hammer.

The four types of hammers: cross peen (A), ball peen (B), straight peen (C), and sledge hammer (D).

There are four basic styles of hammers found in a blacksmith shop:

Cross Peen (A)—Fairly large diameter square face with a peen that looks like a narrow face running perpendicular to the axis of the hammer handle. Weighs 1$\frac{1}{2}$ to 4 pounds (0.7 to 1.8 kg).

Ball Peen (B)—Ball peens have a face that is typically smaller, rounded, and flatter, and weigh less than a cross peen. The most noticeable characteristic is the ball-shaped peen, which can be used to give the surface of hot metal a hammered texture. Weighs 4 ounces to 2$\frac{1}{2}$ pounds (113 g to 1.1 kg).

Straight Peen (C)—This type of hammer has a narrow face that runs parallel to the handle, and typically weighs between 1$\frac{1}{2}$ to 4 pounds (0.7 to 1.8 kg).

Sledge Hammer (D)—This hammer resembles a cross peen but has two faces and no peen. It is heavier than peen hammers. It has a softer face than the peen hammers and is designed for striking cold metal, making it ideal to use with anvil tools. The average hand sledge weighs between 5 and 10 pounds (2.3 to 4.5 kg).

Swing sledges have longer handles and can weigh up to 20 pounds (9 kg), but require an assistant or striker when in use.

A cross peen hammer can also be referred to as a blacksmith hammer, while a sledge hammer is sometimes called an engineer's hammer. When selecting your first forging hammers, I suggest those in the 1$\frac{1}{2}$ to 2$\frac{1}{2}$ pound (0.7 to 1 kg) range. I use a 1$\frac{1}{2}$-pound (1 kg) square face, slightly domed cross peen; a 1$\frac{1}{2}$-pound (1 kg) round face, slightly domed ball peen; and a 4-pound (1.8 kg) handheld sledge.

Eventually, with time and practice, you will want to work with heavier hammers; just be sure to work up slowly. Remember, it's not the size of your hammer that counts, its what you can do with it.

Like new anvils, new hammers need to be dressed; use a grinder to remove the sharp edges from the face to prevent unintentional marking on your metal stock. The grinder marks can then be cleaned up by using a flap disc wheel on the grinder, a belt sander, or a file.

Hammers can be somewhat expensive when bought new, but the supply of used hammers is plentiful.

Before purchasing a used hammer, make sure that the surfaces of the face and peen are smooth and that any existing chips are minor enough to be dressed with a grinder. Large gouges cannot be fixed and should be avoided.

Hammer Handles

A good hammer with a properly fitted handle is mandatory for effective forging—the hammer handle is just as important as the hammer head. The best handles are made from hickory or ash—they are strong woods that do not splinter easily.

When purchasing a new hammer, you will likely need to modify the handle to suit your hand and arm length. If the handle has been varnished, I would recommend sanding off the finish and using linseed oil to seal the wood. Varnish creates a slick finish on wood, and does not provide the best surface area to keep a secure hold. Linseed oil will absorb and protect the wood, but still allows a firm hammer grip.

Lighter weight hammers usually have slightly longer handles than heavier hammers. My forging hammer has a shorter than average handle, and I sanded four faceted edges running the length of it to create a better grip.

Most used hammers will require a new handle. These can be bought at any hardware store. Make sure that the handle is made of a hard wood and that the grain runs the length of the handle—it will be sturdier and less likely to split.

Safety Tip

The hammer most people are familiar with is called a claw or carpenter's hammer. Do not use this style when blacksmithing. Although it may function to move the hot metal, the face is too small and the claw on the opposite end can be dangerous.

Tongs

Tongs are used to move and secure hot metal during the forging process and should be viewed as an extension of your hand. They require coordinated effort and take some practice getting used to. When starting out, you may want to consider keeping your stock long to avoid using tongs. Once you become accustomed to using your hammer hand you can coordinate the other hand's activity of holding stock with tongs.

Like hammers, tongs are available in numerous handle or rein sizes and jaw shapes—each with a specific purpose. It is good to start out with lighter, shorter reined tongs. Longer reins are much harder to learn with, and there is no need to tire your wrist with large heavy tongs. In order to be used effectively, it is essential that you use the appropriate jaw shape for particular shapes of metal stock—the tongs must hold your metal firmly.

Anvil Tools

Anvil tools are also called hardy tools or bottom tools. There are many different types of hardy tools. They all have a square shank attached at the bottom that is inserted into the square hardy hole located on the face of an anvil. Anvil tools need to fit securely into the hardy hole to prevent any movement in the tool while working.

Some anvil tools have a complementing top tool. Top tools perform the same function as their bottom tool counterpart. They are shankless and held directly in your hand. Top and bottom tools can be used in pairs or independent of each other; used together, they manipulate the metal from the top and bottom at the same time, making it much easier to move or cut the metal. Both bottom and top tools are made of high-grade tool steel that is hardened and tempered.

There are six different pairs of tongs that I use on a regular basis:

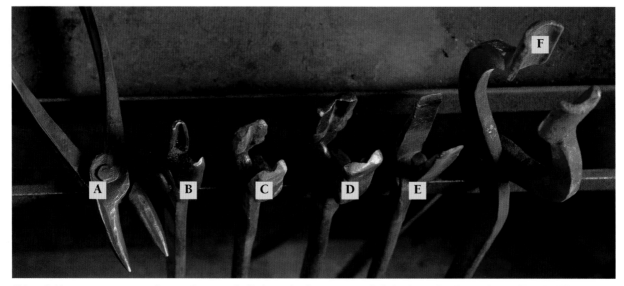

Although I have numerous sets of tongs, there are six distinct pairs that I use on a daily basis. Notice that each set of jaws is different.

OPEN-JAWED TONGS WHICH HOLD DIFFERENT STOCK DIMENSIONS

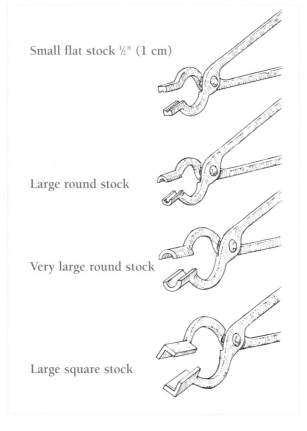

Small flat stock ½" (1 cm)

Large round stock

Very large round stock

Large square stock

Needle Nose or Scroll Tongs (A) are used to refine small curves.

Small Jaw Tongs (B) hold square and round stock 1/4 inch (0.5 cm) or less.

*Small Wolf Jaw Tongs (C) hold round or square stock 1/4 to 1/2 inch (0.5 to 1 cm).

*Large Wolf Jaw Tongs (D) hold round or square stock 1/2 to 5/8 inch (1 to 1.5 cm).

Flat Jaw Tongs (E) hold discs and plate.

Open Jaw Tongs (F) hold stock that already has a forged tip and flat stock.

*While most tongs hold stock parallel to the handles, Wolf Jaw Tongs can hold material in two directions—perpendicular or parallel to the handles.

Tongs can be purchase new or used. When purchasing new tongs, verify with the supplier that they are forged or drop forged rather than cast iron, which can be too brittle. Farm auctions are great place to find used tools. Regardless of how nasty and rusted they appear, old tongs can be reconditioned to suit your needs (i.e., jaws modified to fit a new or unusual shape). Once you begin purchasing, making, and modifying tongs, you will be surprised at how fast your collection will grow.

HOT CUT OR HARDY CHISEL

The hot cut is the most commonly used anvil tool. It is a long, tapered wedge shape that has a cutting edge on the top (see diagram, right). When hot metal is laid across the cutting edge, hammer blows are applied in order to make a deep crevasse, which will eventually cut the metal stock apart.

Just as the name implies, the hot cut is used to separate a section of metal from the parent stock. The hot cut tool fits into the hardy hole and has an elongated taper to either a centered edge or an offset edge. The offset hardy chisel produces a cleaner cut, but both styles work in the same way.

COLD CUT

Like the hot cut, the purpose of the cold cut is to separate lengths of stock from its parent. The cold cut can be used on unheated pieces of metal. The shape of the cold cut is wide and squat, with less of a tapered point leading to its edge.

This hardy tool is more compact and stout than the hot cut. The cutting edge of the cold cut has a much steeper angle than the hot cut. Cold cuts are generally used for cutting original lengths of material when it is purchased from the supplier—10 or 20 foot (3.2 or 6.1 m) lengths.

As you would expect, cold cutting metal is more difficult because you are cutting into a hard material—more pressure and accuracy is needed to split the stock.

HOT AND COLD ANVIL TOOLS

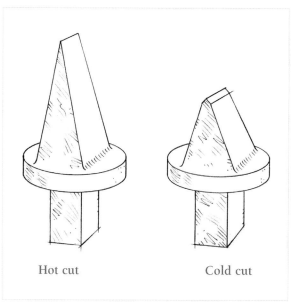

Hot cut   Cold cut

Notice the difference between the tool shapes and cutting edges of the hot cut and cold cut anvil tools.

A working blacksmith's tong rack fills up quickly.

FULLER

A fuller, whether it is a hardy fuller with a square shank that fits into the hardy hole or a hand-held spring fuller, is a basic tool that is used to start many blacksmithing projects. Despite its name, a fuller is used to make your material thinner, and its edge radius is used to move the stock material in rounded grooves. The radius of the fuller determines the radius of the grooved notches. Fullers have very blunt and rounded edges and are available in numerous shapes and sizes. Although their wedge shape resembles the hot and cold cuts, fullers do not have a cutting edge.

A hardy fuller will shape only one side of the stock material unless it is rotated to establish a fuller mark around the perimeter of the stock. Some hardy fullers come with a matching top fuller—a handled chisel with the same radius shape that mimics the hardy fuller.

SWAGE

A swage (pronounced swedge) is a finishing tool with a concave depression that is used to refine a shape that has been initially formed by other forging techniques. Like fullers, swages are available in numerous shapes and sizes and can be used singularly or in pairs. Swages can be a hardy tool, a handled set, or a spring set.

GUILLOTINE

A guillotine tool has the properties of both the hardy and spring fuller. The tool itself fits into the hardy hole and it has a top and bottom dye used to form metal similar to a spring set. The guillotine tool offers many benefits to the solo smith. Its design is like that of top and bottom tooling, but the pieces are held in place by an angle iron bracket, which frees up your hands to rotate and hammer the stock. The upper or top die can be lowered onto hot stock that is resting on the bottom die. There are commercial guillotine tools available but one can also be made with the assistance of an electric welder. Directions for making one are in Chapter Seven.

Different types of anvil tools provide the blacksmith with particular function.

HARDY BENDING FORK

A hardy bending fork allows a smith to see the curve during the bending process (see photo, page 32). The square shank holds a small plate with two pegs on top. Metal stock is inserted between the two pegs and leverage is applied. This tool allows the smith to create very isolated curves on a piece of metal stock.

There is also a hand held version of this tool—it is simply called a bending fork. Instructions for making a hardy bending fork and a hand held bending fork are in Chapter Seven.

—⚒—

I particularly like using a hardy bending fork when creating scrolls. The opening in the fork allows you to see the curve as it is being created over the anvil face. If you use the horn or the edge of the anvil for scrolling, your view is impeded by the anvil's mass.

—⚒—

Trick of the Trade

Spring tools are top and bottom dies that are connected with a handle on one end to allow for a spring-like movement. A spring set allows you to shape two opposing sides of stock material with each hammer blow.

When hammering manually, spring sets are generally used with the help of a striker. They can be used solo under a fly press or power hammer.

If a hardy shaft is welded to the bottom die of the spring set, it becomes a hardy tool, which can be used while hammering manually at your anvil without the assistance of a striker.

A hardy spring fuller was used to shape this piece of round stock.

SWAGE AND FULLER SETS

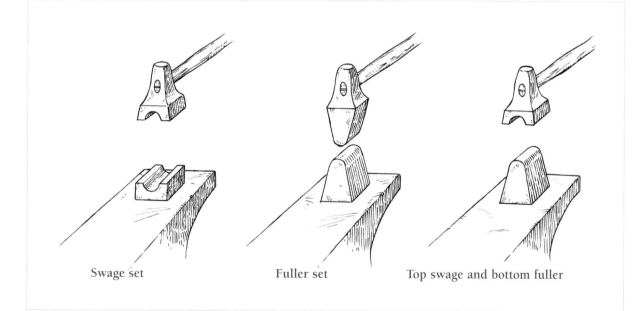

Swage set   Fuller set   Top swage and bottom fuller

This illustration depicts how top and bottom fullers and swages can be used to shape metal. They can be used together or interchangeably.

A hardy bending fork allows the blacksmith to create isolated curves.

HEADER

A header is a bottom tool used to make heads on nails, rivets, and bolts. It is a thick bar of tool steel with tapered holes of different diameters. A nail header has a raised face that allows for decorative angled hammer blows and a rounded finish on the head of the nail. A bolt header has a flat face since bolts have flat heads.

MANDREL

A mandrel is an anvil tool used to form circular shapes and rings. When a mandrel is bent at an angle, it is called an anvil beak because it is a smaller version the beak horn found on your anvil.

Cone mandrels can be small in size with a shaft that fits inside the hardy hole, or they can be large and freestanding, up to 4 feet (1.2 m) high, and weigh hundreds of pounds.

The purpose of this tapered cone shape is to true up circular shapes such as rings. Some cone mandrels have a slot running lengthwise, which is used to accommodate a pair of tongs holding the stock piece.

CUTTING PLATE

Cutting plates can be placed directly on your anvil face or held more securely using a hardy insert. The plate should be at least 1/4 inch (0.5 cm) thick and constructed of soft steel. As mentioned earlier, I use a piece of 1/4 inch (0.5 cm)-thick copper that is laid directly on the anvil face. A plate should be used whenever there is the possibility of a sharp tool edge making contact with your anvil; it is much easier to sharpen a tool edge than to resurface your anvil.

ROLL BAR

I made this tool specifically because my anvil does not have a step down or a cutting table. It is used to initiate the process of rolling or curling flat stock lengthwise. Directions for making a roll bar are in Chapter Seven.

Handheld Tools

Although all of your hammers will have handles, there are other common hand held tools used during the forging process that are available with or without handles.

The benefit of a handle is that it provides a safe distance between your hand and the radiant heat coming off of the stock. It also allows a safe distance between your hand and your hammer swing.

The drawback of handled tools is that they create more distance between the smith and the work being forged. Many handled tools require a striker or assistant—one person holds the tooling in place, while the other hammers.

It seems to be much easier for a novice smith to use non-handled tools—these tools are easier to manipulate and strike accurately. Non-handled tools allow for you to get closer to your work. I would suggest using handheld punches and chisels measuring at least 10 inches (25 cm) long. A gloved hand will allow you to grip these tools comfortably and reduce the chance of being burnt.

Make sure that the tooling is held perpendicular to the metal stock when striking. The flat surface of the hand tool should run parallel to the flat surface of the anvil. If the tooling is angled and the hammer lands on the flat surface at an angle, the impact could make the tool fly out of your hand, leaving your bare hand exposed with no barrier to stop the hammer or the hot piece of metal from making contact with your skin.

Safety Tip

Remember, *never* use your forging hammer to make impact on a hand tool. Forging hammers should only make contact with heated metal stock, not other tools. Use a light sledge or another hammer that you do not mind getting marred when striking hand tools.

CHISEL

Chisels are easy tools to make. They are used for cutting, veining, and carving. Each chisel is made to perform a different task or to make a specific mark in the metal.

PUNCH

Punches are made with a variety of tips—round, square, oval, and rectangle—and it is the first tool used when creating holes in hot metal stock. The advantage of punching holes, rather than using a drill, is the minimal amount of material lost in the process.

When setting up your shop, it is good to have a least one round, one square, and one center punch. When using a punch, the final blows, the ones that will push out the pellet, are centered over the pritchel hole; this will ensure that the face of your anvil is protected. After the pellet is punched out of the stock, the stock is then ready for a drift to be passed through.

Safety Tip

During the punching process, dip the tip of your punch into water after every couple of blows; this will keep the tip cool and reduce the possibility of tempering the punch.

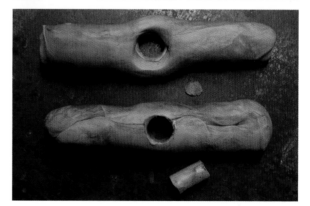

These two pieces of clay demonstrate the material that is preserved when holes are punched, rather than drilled. The top piece of clay was punched. A small pellet of material was removed, and the punched area appears swelled. The bottom piece shows that a smaller amount of material is lost when the hole is drilled.

DRIFT

Drifts are used to open up and shape the hole that has been punched out of the stock. Drifts can be round, square, rectangle, oval, and even hexagonal, and are usually only applied to heated metal. The drift has a long taper on one end and a short taper on the other. The long taper is the part that pushes through the slot, and the opening is then finished by hammering through to the short taper. Your goal is to hammer the drift completely through the metal stock (over the pritchel hole), thus creating the desired size hole.

CUPPING TOOL OR RIVET SET

A cupping tool or rivet set is a finishing tool used to clean up the head of a rivet. The companion to the cupping tool is the rivet set, which is placed on the bottom side of the rivet being formed so that it will not flatten the head on the opposite side.

Coal Forge Tools

- **Shovels** are used to add fuel to the fire as well as to shape the fire.
- **Pokers** are used to poke holes into an accumulated coal mass and also to separate your fire by-products.
- **Rakes** are used to maintain the contents of your fire bed.
- **Watering cans** are used to control an active fire. Water is used to **coke** the fire and control the size of your fire. Water is much cheaper than coal, and when applied appropriately, it will save fuel costs.

Coal Forge

A forge is basically defined as an open hearth used by smiths to contain their fire. They are available in a wide variety of shapes and sizes, but all coal forges consist of the same components. Modern coal forges are almost identical to ones used thousands of years ago. (See diagram, next page).

A gloved hand allows you to comfortably and safely grip non-handled tools.

It is a good idea to have different handles on all of your forge tools so each one can be identified by its handle. Sometimes it is difficult for your eyes to adjust quickly from the fire to the forge table, and this will help you grab the intended tool with just a glance.

ANATOMY OF A COAL FORGE

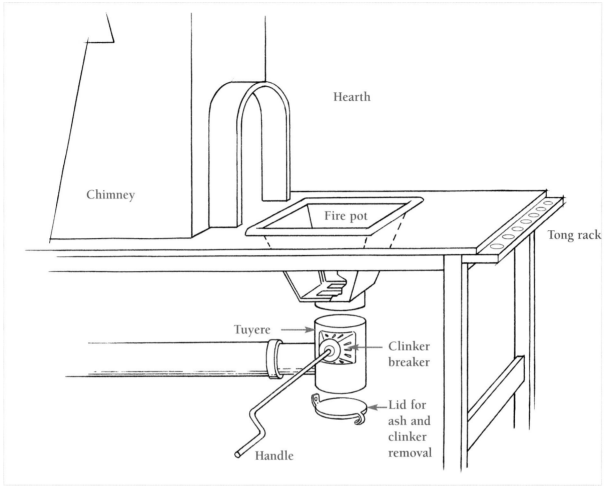

This illustration depicts the inside of the hearth and the tuyere.

There are five basic tools necessary to help maintain a coal forge fire: Rake (A), Poker (B), Flux spoon (C), Water can (D), and Coal shovel (E).

FIRE POT AND HEARTH

The hearth is the structure that holds the fire pot and chimney in place. It is made from plate steel 3/16 to 3/8 inches (4.5 mm to 1 cm) thick, depending on its overall size. The hearth should have enough space to store extra coal and a rack for tongs.

TUYERE

Through the tuyere, forced air enters the fire box and creates the heat needed for forging. The amount of air directed into the fire controls the size and character of the fire. The most basic tuyere is a pipe with holes punched in the middle: one end is plugged and the other attached to the blower. It is installed so that the fire will be built over the holes. It is important to keep the vent clear of any debris or else you will lose air flow. A tuyere can be located on the side or bottom of the fire box.

HOOD AND CHIMNEY

The function of the hood is to remove smoke and gases from the workspace. An exhaust fan can be connected to the top of your chimney to remove the smoke and gases efficiently. Hoods may be located over the top of the hearth or to the side of the hearth by the chimney. If installing the hood above the hearth, do not place it too low or else you will not be able to produce a draft. Do not install it too high or else it will lose its ability to collect polluted air. Make sure that your chimney or exhaust pipe is linear or has as few bends as possible.

BLOWER

The purpose of a blower is to supply air to the fire; this will increase the amount of fuel being consumed, resulting in a more intense heat. A hand-pumped blower is called a bellow. Bellows are wood and leather "lungs" that pull air into its two chambers and then force the air out of the lungs into the fire pot. They are rarely seen in today's shops but were used before the advent of the hand-cranked squirrel cage or electric blowers.

Blowers may be mechanically geared or an independent mechanism can be attached to your forge to produce the airflow. It is essential that you are able to control the amount of air because airflow controls the rate of combustion and fire temperature. A rheostat for the electric blower or a damper will help control these variables.

Additional Tools and Equipment

All of these items are universally found in blacksmith shops. Some of them are essential, such as quench bucket, vise, and wire brush, and others will make your smithy a much more functional work space and you a much more productive smith.

QUENCH BUCKET

The quench bucket is a container of water used for cooling hot metal. Water may also be used during the heat treating process. The bucket should actually be tub-sized as the container needs to be large enough to immerse metal stock in it. Wood or metal make the best containers. Do not use a plastic container since this material can be easily punctured with a hot piece of metal.

Most shops use wooden planter half-barrels, which can be found at garden centers and greenhouse retailers. The tub's wood needs to soak up water and expand so that you will have a waterproof seal. To create this seal, fill a new barrel full of water and leave it

> ### Trick of the Trade
> Because of its weight, I keep my swage block on its own stand (log stump) so any lifting of the block is limited to simply rotating or flipping it. The wood stump works well for securing the swage block, especially on its edge. I drive tapered pegs into the wood to secure the block in any position.

outside your shop area. Keep adding water every hour or so, until the wood begins to expand and it stops leaking. Let it stand a day or two, refilling with water as necessary. Once the leaking stops, simply empty the tub and relocate it to the desired space in your shop, and refill it to the top. Keep your quench bucket full, otherwise the wood will dry and lose its ability to hold water.

VISE

The vise is used to secure metal stock when it is being hammered or bent, making it a vital piece of equipment for your work space. The vise can also be used to secure and use anvil tools that do not properly fit into your anvil's hardy hole. In general, vises are described by the length of their jaws, such as 4 inch (10 cm) vise, 5 inch (13 cm) vise, and so on.

There are two basic types of vises:

• **Bench or Machinist Vise**—This vise should be securely mounted to a flat work surface. It has detachable jaws that remain parallel to each other when the vise is open or closed.

• **Leg or Post Vise**—This is a floor-standing vise with forged steel jaws that are hinged so that they pivot on an arc. This type of vise is much more durable than a bench vise. The leg provides additional stability as the force of pressure is applied to the floor.

When purchasing a new vise, check the jaws to see if they have a grip pattern on the clamping surface. You will need to grind off the pattern so that marks will not be made on a hot piece of metal stock. Because the jaws of a bench vise are removable, you can replace the hardened steel textured jaws with smooth mild steel jaws, or you can drop in sleeves of softer metal, like copper, that will hug the material securely but not mar it.

When purchasing a used vise, make sure to check that the jaws are operable. Screw them completely open and shut to ensure that the clamping screw is not damaged. Examine the screw assembly carefully. If the threads are heavily worn or broken, you should pass on buying the vise since this is difficult to repair. If the old vise appears to be frozen or locked up, there is probably an accumulation of rust in the threads. Sometimes heat or chemical lubricants and solvents can be used to recondition the threads.

WIRE BRUSH

Keep a constant supply of wire brushes on hand while at work. They are used to remove scale during the forging process. Fire scale is a natural by-product of heated mild steel, so brushing needs to become a normal part of your routine. If you do not remove these impurities from the stock surface before forging, they will embed into the surface of metal stock and cause pitting.

I have a post vise that is permanently attached to the concrete floor (right) and a second vise that is portable.

Wire brushing is also important for safety reasons. If not removed before forging, scale may pop off under the impact of your hammer blows, resulting in black, hot flakes of metal being embedded into your flesh. Red hot metal cauterizes and bounces off the flesh. Black hot metal sticks to the skin while burning.

SWAGE BLOCK

This swage block is a block of cast steel that has many different depressions on all six sides. The two faces have concave round and oval shapes ranging in size and depth. The edges have grooves varying in width and depth.

The swage block can be laid directly on the face of the anvil when needed, so some smiths consider the swage block to be an anvil tool.

Swage blocks are not necessary for the beginner smith, but like all tooling, once you see how it works and helps, you'll wonder how you ever lived without it.

Magic Elixir

An wise old man told me that the water in a quench bucket was the best cure-all for poison ivy that he had ever used. When a friend came down with a bad case of poison ivy and told me that calamine lotion wasn't working, I shared the wise man's story. She promptly filled a plastic spray bottle with my dirty quench water and coated her arms and legs. A day later she returned to the shop wanting to sell the "magic elixir" to the public.

The theory? Heavy concentrations of iron in the water accelerated the drying up of poison ivy blisters.

Trick of the Trade

Adding a brass wire brush to your collection will give you the option of coloring a forged piece. The warm metal of your finished piece can be scrubbed with the soft brass bristles. The brass will actually coat the steel's surface. This process is called burnishing.

ADJUSTABLE STAND

An adjustable stand is essential for blacksmiths who are working alone. It is basically a tripod stand that allows for different pieces to be inserted. U-shaped stands prevent stock from rolling off and some have rollers which allow for stock to be slid backwards and forwards. Stands work well for propping up long pieces of stock in the forge and to help in positioning stock that is to be forged at your anvil.

The best time to wire brush heated metal stock is when it has a bright orange color temperature.

FILES

Files are used to remove burrs and sharp edges from your ironwork. With delicate use, a file can smooth out the surface of your stock. Files need careful use as overdoing it may leave bright scratch marks on the surface. If this should happen, simply reheat the metal to a red heat temperature color as the metal will oxidize and "hide" the scratches.

In general, files should be used on cold stock, but a specific type of file, called a farrier's file or rasp, is much coarser than regular steel-working files and can be used on hot metal.

Marking and Measuring Tools

SOAPSTONE

A soapstone pencil is great for general marking purposes and can be used on your floor shop to draw out guide plans for pieces you are forging. Regular blackboard chalk has a relatively low melting temperature and is not well suited for use in a shop.

CENTER PUNCH

Earlier in this chapter I mentioned punches. There is a particular punch with a tapered tip called a center punch, and it is used to mark hole placement in cold metal before using a larger punch.

SCRIBER AND DIVIDER

A scriber is a sharp pointed tool used to scratch lines into cold metal. Although this is a specific tool, a sharp prick punch can also be used to perform this function. A divider is a metal instrument used for marking or measuring. It can be used to mark arcs or circles, and to divide lengths into equal sections.

SQUARE

The square is an instrument that has a 90 degree angle and two straight edges. It is used to mark and verify straight edges or any specified angle measurements.

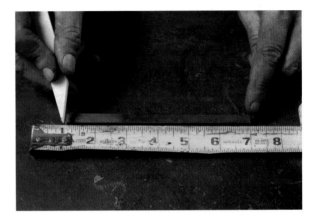

SAFETY TIP

When collecting measuring tools for your shop, it is advisable to steer clear of any instruments not made of metal since other materials can be singed or burnt. Stainless steel and chrome-plated measuring tools are excellent because they do not rust.

The metal tab on most tape measures is not securely attached, which may result in imprecise measurements. Use the 1 inch (2.5 cm) mark as the starting point for measuring stock. Just remember to subtract 1 inch (2.5 cm) from your final measurement.

Use a soapstone pencil to draw a sketch on the floor or work table. Use the cloth tape measure to help in calculating the amount of stock needed to make that shape.

RULERS AND TAPE MEASURES

A 2 foot (0.6 m) long metal ruler and a 20 foot (6.1 m) tape measure are the standard tools for measuring.

The one exception is that I use a cloth tape measure to determine the circumference of a pipe or the length of stock needed to form a scroll. Cloth measuring tapes are used on cold metal only.

Modern Technology

Throughout history, blacksmiths have continually designed and built things to make their jobs easier. Blacksmiths have been good at modernizing the craft by improving tools, materials, and equipment.

Traditionally, hand-forged ironwork has become the exception, rather than normal, practice. The use of modern equipment is not cheating, but there are smiths who only use the traditional technologies of hammer, forge, and anvil when creating their work. Blacksmithing conferences demonstrate just how vast and all encompassing this craft and its practitioners truly are.

As an artist, my goal is to use whatever tool or piece of equipment that is available to help me create the finished product. As a business person, I am expected to make or repair things as efficiently as possible. Over the years, I have been able to accumulate modern equipment. There will always be other shops with more toys, but what I have allows me to do everything I want to. As stated before, some of my equipment was purchased new, and some of it was obtained through auctions.

BAND SAW

This is used for making controlled cuts through thin sheets and smaller stock sizes. A slow and accurate cutting method, the teeth rotate downward as the material is pushed through. The material can be secured into the vise with the blade arm rotated downward to make the cut.

BELT SANDER

I use a 1 inch (2.5 cm) belt sander for refining tiny areas of shapes that are plasma cut, as well as finishing the edges of blades and sharpening tools. The 4 inch (10 cm) belt sander is much more aggressive, and it is used to grind metal away quickly. Belt sanders are classified by the size of the belt being used. The grit of the belt determines the aggressiveness.

Fun Fact:
MIG and TIG Welders

A MIG (Metal Inert Gas) welder employs a coil of aluminum alloy wire that acts as the electrode and filler material. It is a welding process that joins metals by heating them with an arc. No metal is transferred across the arc; metal is deposited only when the wire touches the metal piece you are working on.

A TIG (Tungsten Insert Gas) welder joins metals by heating them with a tungsten electrode, which does not become part of the weld. Filler metal is usually used, though it is possible to weld without it.

ELECTRIC WELDERS

The wire welder is the most commonly used because it needs very small wires (.035 inch or about 1 mm) and welding with it requires very little clean up. The buzz box is a small portable stick welder that I can roll out of the shop to repair trailers, hitches, and other rusty stuff.

My shop is equipped with a Miller MIG wire welder; an old, small Lincoln buzz box; and a really old, rather large, Miller welder that is set up for stick and TIG welding. Contact a dealer or supply company to better explain the different kinds of welders.

As I write this book, I am in the process of learning TIG welding process.

Band saw

Belt sander

Chop saw

MIG welder

CHOP SAW

The chop saw's abrasive disc rotates at high speed, cutting heavy stock quicker than a band saw. The drawbacks are the loud cutting sounds and the grit that flies off during the cutting process. They also have a tendency to leave a hot, sharp burr on the cut edge, which needs to be sanded away before handling.

DRILL PRESS

It is so much easier to use a drill press, rather than a hand held drill. I have an adjustable vise mounted to the table of my drill press, which secures the metal while drilling. If you already have one in your shop, it is advisable to get another. Two drill presses allow you to have different speeds and bits for pilot drilling, countersinking, and large bit drilling.

GAS FORGE

There are many benefits to having a gas forge. Gas forges can be built to fit any shape, they produce longer heats on stock, and they can be adapted to work with propane or natural gas. The gas forge allows you to have several pieces of stock heating without the risk of burning them. The gas forge is a cleaner heat source than coal.

—ᴡᴡ—

With so many advantages offered with the gas forge, why the coal forge is still around? First of all, there is nothing that connects you with this craft more than fire. A coal fire can be made anywhere and the intensity of the heat makes forge welding, upsetting, and punch/drifting easier to execute. A coal fire represents the history of the craft.

—ᴡᴡ—

HANDHELD GRINDERS

Having a collection of 4 1/2- and 5-inch (11 and 13 cm) hand grinders saves a lot of time in cleaning up and finishing ironwork. It is not uncommon to have a half-dozen of them with different disc grits, wheels, and brush cups on hand.

**Fun Fact:
The Fourth State of Matter**
Plasma cutters are similar to lightening in that they move electricity from one place to another. Plasma is often referred to as the fourth state of matter. When a solid is continuously heated, it turns into liquid, then into a gas, and finally into plasma—an electrically conductive gas.

Although gas forges are available commercially, I built my own.

Handheld grinders

I use Daisy Mae everyday—a 50# Mayer Bros. trip hammer

My Beau—circa 1920, 150# Beaudry trip hammer

PEDESTAL GRINDER

These are stationary machines that have two thick stone grinding wheels, one on each side of the motor. They are used for shaping, grinding, and sharpening iron.

MECHANICAL HAMMER

My two trip hammers are both very old and can move more metal in a fraction of the time it takes to do by hand. Think of a power hammer as a mechanical arm that never gets tired.

PLASMA CUTTER

The plasma cutter uses electricity and compressed air to cut through metal. It cuts metal as fast as you can draw or move the gun. There are many affordable plasma cutters on the market today. The main draw-back to this piece of equipment is the exhaust and particulate matter that is released. It requires adequate ventilation and protective masks to filter the air.

Blacksmith Networking

The Artist Blacksmith Association of North America (ABANA) and its local chapter groups offer magazines, newsletters, and online bulletin boards that allow members to advertise the sale and trade of equipment. By joining your local affiliate, you will expand your network of resources and knowledge. In addition to discussing tools and equipment, these groups offer educational opportunities by hosting hammer-ins (blacksmithing demonstrations), providing how-to project instructions, promoting upcoming black-smithing events and conferences, and pub-lishing information about the various schools and private shops that offer classes.

CHAPTER THREE

IRON

Although it has always been abundant in its natural state as iron ore, the use of iron was very limited until humans learned how to smelt it. Iron ore comprises iron, manganese, oxygen phosphorus, silicon, and sulfur. Smelting is a technically sophisticated process that reduces metal ore using a chemical reaction that occurs when the ore is subjected to high temperatures. When impurities are removed from iron ore, either cast iron or a semi-pasty bloom of wrought iron is created.

Today, contemporary blacksmiths often use the terms iron and steel interchangeably. This chapter will cover rudimentary information about iron, iron steel, and what to expect when you make your first visit to the steel yard to pick up stock materials.

What is Iron?

Iron is the fourth most plentiful element in the world and comprises more than 5 percent of the Earth's crust. It is a metallic element that is malleable and magnetic and it is identified by its silvery-white appearance. The atomic number of iron is 26, its symbol is Fe, and its name is derived from the Latin word ferrum.

In order to extract iron from iron ore, the ore is heated in a furnace. Upon heating, oxygen molecules release from the ore and attach themselves to airborne carbon monoxide molecules, thus forming carbon dioxide. This process transforms the iron ore into a porous, spongy mass of iron and impurities—the remaining mass is called a bloom. Through repeated heating and hammering, the impurities, termed slag, are excised form the mass and the remaining metallic particles are condensed, resulting in iron.

Iron alloys, not iron, are the materials used by blacksmiths today. Iron alloys are either a combination of iron and other metals, or they comprise metals and non-metallic elements.

CHARACTERISTICS OF STEEL

All of these terms are used to describe the properties of steel:

Brittleness—The tendency of metal to fracture or break with little or no hammering, bending, or twisting.

Compressive strength—The ability of a metal to withstand pressures acting on a given plane.

Corrosion resistance—The resistance to being eroded by air, moisture, or other environmental factors.

Ductility—The ability of a metal to be drawn or stretched permanently without rupture or fracture.

Hardness—The ability of a metal to resist penetration and wear by another metal or material.

Elasticity—The ability of metal to return to its original size and shape after being stretched or pulled out of shape.

Machinability and Weldability—The ease or difficulty with which metal can be machined or welded.

Malleability—The ability of a metal to be hammered, rolled, or pressed into various shapes without rupture or fracture.

Shear strength—The ability of a metal to resist being fractured by opposing forces not acting in a straight line.

Tensile strength—The ability of a metal to resist being pulled apart by opposing forces in a straight line.

Toughness—The ability of a metal to resist fracture plus its ability to resist failure after the damage has been done.

The most prominent iron alloy is steel, which is a combination of iron and carbon. Steel is graded or classified by its carbon content. The malleability, ductility, and weldability of steel decreases as the carbon content increases.

The metallurgy of steel production was not formally studied until the later half of the nineteenth century. For centuries prior, metalworkers used carbon while smelting iron without any documented scientific alchemy formulas. A blacksmith judged the quality of his materials intuitively through observable traits such as appearance, texture, and grain.

Wrought Iron

Wrought iron is a mixture of pure iron and iron silicate that contains 0.02 to 0.08 percent carbon. It is considered the traditional material of blacksmiths, but it is no longer widely produced due to the intensive labor required to manufacture it. There are a few specialty mills in Europe that manufacture wrought iron, but the prices are somewhat expensive. Some blacksmiths search for old scrap wrought iron and recycle it into modern uses.

The actual word "wrought" means to create something through the expenditure of labor, such as hammering by hand or machine, and usually implies a degree of decoration.

In order to produce wrought iron, pig iron is heated until all of the carbon and impurities are burned off. The remaining mass is hammered, milled, reheated, and silicon slag is added. Wrought iron, cast iron, and steel are all made from pig iron.

Wrought iron has fibrous characteristics similar to wood—it will split and crack along its grain lines. It can be forged at a yellow heat, and any attempt at a lower temperature color will result in the metal splitting like a wooden board. Wrought iron is rust and corrosion resistant—it will rust down to the iron silicate and then stop.

Wrought iron can be converted into steel. The process is called steeling, and it entails heating the wrought iron, repeatedly hammering it to remove slag and other impurities, reheating it in a charcoal fire to allow carbon absorption into the metal, quenching it to achieve hardness, and tempering.

THE MODERN DEFINITION OF WROUGHT IRON

These days, the term wrought iron is not used to describe the material. Modern usage of the term is interchangeable with the term forged iron— the process of heating iron and working it by hand hammering over an anvil.

Because there is so much mass-produced wrought iron made throughout the world, today's blacksmiths refer to their work as "hand-wrought," which means that it is hand-forged.

Cast Iron

Cast iron is not forged, so it is not a product of the blacksmith, but cast iron products are used extensively, so I've included some general information about the material.

The development of the process of casting iron is considered one the greatest technical contributions of the Middle Ages. Smiths extended their techniques of casting bronze to casting the much more abundant cast iron. The ability to cast iron made a strong and comparatively inexpensive metal available to the mass market, instead of the more expensive wrought iron and crucible steel bars, which were beaten into strips and laminated into tools and weapons.

Cast iron is an alloy of iron, carbon, and silicon, and it contains approximately 2.0 and 3.0 percent carbon. It is created by melting pig iron with small amounts of scrap iron. The molten metal is then poured into molds and allowed to solidify. Cast iron is extremely popular because it is inexpensive and can be poured into numerous shapes.

Cast iron, however, is hard and brittle and cannot be bent. When metal contains more than 2.0 percent carbon, it loses it ductility—it cannot be forged, forge welded, or tempered. If cast iron is heated to a red color temperature and hit with a hammer, it will crumble.

What is Steel?

Steel is an alloy of iron, carbon, and small proportions of manganese, phosphorus, sulfur, and silicon. When iron is smelted from iron ore, it contains more carbon than desirable. To become steel, it must be melted and reprocessed to remove the correct amount of carbon. The carbon content of steel makes it more durable and harder than softer wrought iron, and more resistant to tension than brittle cast iron.

CARBON STEEL

When steel is classified by its carbon content, typically ranging between 0.10 to 2.10 percent, it is referred to as carbon steel. The optimum strength for carbon steel is achieved at 0.40 to 0.45 percent carbon.

All steel contains carbon, but the term carbon steel refers to steel that contains carbon as its primary alloy. Although it may seem insignificant, small differences in the amount of carbon greatly affects the quality of steel.

Mild or Low Carbon Steel	0.10 to 0.25 percent
Medium Carbon Steel	0.25 to 0.45 percent
High Carbon Steel	0.45 to 0.95 percent
Very High Carbon Steel	0.95 to 2.10 percent

MILD OR LOW CARBON STEEL

Mild or low carbon steel is the most common grade of steel used by blacksmiths today, and it is the primary steel discussed and used in this book. (High carbon steel is the primary material used for the projects in Chapter Seven: How to Make Your Own Tooling).

Mild or low carbon steel is also referred to as soft steel, machine steel, or blacksmith iron. It is made by removing practically all of the carbon from pig iron. There is not enough carbon to allow hardening by heating and quenching it in water. It can be bent and hammered cold to some extent and can be forged and forge welded.

IRON

47

ALLOY STEEL

Although all steel is an alloy and all steel contains carbon, the term "alloy steel" refers to steel that contains elements other than carbon as its primary alloy. Interest in developing alloy metals increased significantly during World War II, when increased metal strength was tantamount for war machine production. The most common alloy elements are chromium, aluminum, nickel, and tungsten.

Stainless steel is an alloy steel that most of us are familiar with. Because of its high chromium content, stainless has a high tensile strength and is resistant to abrasion and corrosion.

THE SPARK TEST OF STEEL

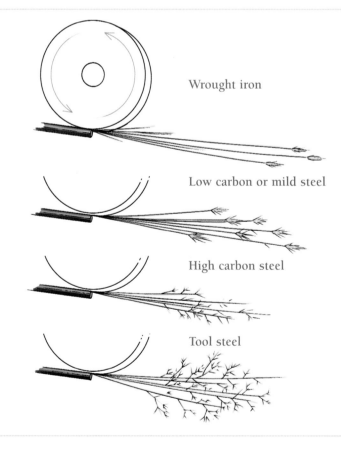

Wrought iron

Low carbon or mild steel

High carbon steel

Tool steel

A good way to distinguish between various grades of steel is to grind them on a grinding wheel and note the sparks that are given off. Sparks from wrought iron are light yellow or red and follow straight lines. Sparks from mild steel are similar but more explosive. High carbon steel gives off sparks that are lighter in color and still more explosive. The higher the percentage of carbon in the steel, the brighter and more explosive the sparks.

Steel stock is available in a multitude of shapes and sizes. Purchase your stock material from your local supplier.

Commercial Forms of Steel

When learning how to forge metal, I encourage you to purchase your steel stock from your local steelyard or mill. It is not recommended to learn how to forge using scrap materials since you will be unsure as to what types of steel you are working with and their properties.

Steel stock is available in a multitude of shapes: Angle, Bar, Channel, Foil, Half-Round, Hexagon, I Beam, L Shape, Octagon, Pipe, Plate, Rectangle, Round, Sheet, Square, Strip, Tee, Tube, Wire, and Wire Mesh.

The lengths of stock can vary anywhere between 8 to 24 feet (2.4 to 7.3 m). Your local steel supplier will cut the stock for you at whatever lengths you specify. I typically have my stock cut in half, up to 10 feet (3 m) in length, which allows me to transport it in the back of my pickup truck.

SAFETY TIP

Always bring red cautionary flags with you when you take a trip to the steelyard. The flags should be attached to the ends of any metal stock that protrudes from your vehicle 3 feet (100 cm) or more.

The most common types of mild steel stock you will work with are round and square stock. Mild steel is processed in two distinct ways—hot rolled and cold rolled.

The basic difference between hot rolled and cold rolled steel is that hot rolled steel is rolled to its final dimensions while hot enough to scale (over 1700°F or 850°C) and cold rolled steel is rolled to its final dimensions well below scaling temperature.

Hot rolled steel—is carbon steel that is rolled at a mill and left with a scaled finish. It is not heat-treated and is referred to as HR—"hot roll." The edges of hot rolled square and rectangular stock are somewhat rounded.

Cold rolled steel—is heat-treated and the finished product is more precise than hot rolled. When milled cold, the final product is compacted and strengthened, with crisp edges. Referred to as CF—cold finished.

Because of the additional labor required to make cold rolled steel, it is more expensive to purchase than hot rolled. Use the more affordable hot rolled steel. Cold rolled steel will not provide you with any particular advantage as you are learning how to forge metal.

—⚒—

It is always a good idea to keep a supply of stock available in your shop. If you are unable to transport materials from the steel yard, ask the supplier if they can deliver the stock to you.

—⚒—

CHAPTER FOUR

PRELIMINARY SKILLS

Now that you have assembled the blacksmithing tools and set up your workspace, there are a few simple, yet essential tasks that need to be addressed before you begin forging. The following information and preparatory skills provide a foundation for you to work efficiently and effectively in your smithy.

Coal

Coal is a combustible organic rock largely composed of carbon, hydrogen, and oxygen, with variable amounts of mineral matter. This fossil fuel was formed from decomposed plants that were compressed beneath Earth's surface for millions of years. It is believed that prehistoric vegetation accumulated at the bottom of swamps and was buried by the shifting of the earth's tectonic plates. Once below ground, pressure and high temperatures transformed the rotting materials into coal. Most coal mined today was formed during the Carboniferous Period, which spanned 290 to 360 million years ago.

Coal is graded into different ranks based upon its hardness, moisture content, and combustibility. These variables are dependent upon the temperatures and pressures a coal deposit has been subjected to, as well as the length of time the deposit has been forming.

The most common fuel used in a blacksmith's coal forge is bituminous coal, often referred to as green or raw coal. Bituminous is a soft-grade coal and it can be purchased from various suppliers and coal yards. The burning of bituminous coal creates two by-products: coke and clinkers.

Coke is a term used for purified coal. It is the porous residue that forms after the sulfur and other impurities have burned out of the coal. It is an excellent heat source that provides a very clean burn. Coke is a fusion of carbon and residual ash that results when bituminous coal is burned and is grey in appearance.

Coke can be purchased from a retailer, but after you light and burn your first coal fire, you will have begun to create a supply of coke. When you start up a coal fire, you are simultaneously creating the heat source for the iron and also turning the coal into coke. At the end of your forging, the burnt coal and coke that remains in the forge will be used to start your next fire.

Clinkers are gummy, solidified wastes comprising the impurities that accumulate as you continue to burn coal. The key to recognizing a clinker from a piece of coal is that a hot clinker is sticky and clumpy, while a hot piece of coal remains porous. Clinkers, because of their weight, will naturally sink to the bottom of the fire pot and obstruct the tuyere, which provides the airflow in your forge.

—⁂—

As a beginner blacksmith, I was constantly trying to figure out why my coal forge would not keep a good heat after about an hour of forging. Upon taking my first blacksmithing class, I was awarded a blue ribbon for the largest clinker donut—it weighed almost a pound. Everyone was amazed that I had been able to maintain any fire with such a build-up of wastes.

—⁂—

While the forge is in use, an occasional poke into the bottom of the fire bed and a slight shifting around of the surrounding area will expose the glowing clinkers. Simply pick them out using your fire poker or tongs.

Different Ranks of Coal

LIGNITE (Brown coal)	Contains a lot of moisture and ash and breaks apart easily. Of the four types, lignite has the lowest carbon content and heating value.
SUB-BITUMINOUS	Is dull black in appearance and has less moisture than lignite.
BITUMINOUS (Hard coal)	Contains very little moisture and has high heat value. It is used to produce coke.
ANTHRACITE	Contains the highest carbon content and the lowest moisture and ash content.

This was yesterday's coal fire. You can see a nice collection of the remains of the burning process. Next to the chimney is coke and ash, in the center is coke, and to the right, green coal. The light clumps in the foreground are the clinkers that came from the bottom of the fire pot.

Fire Tending

The most time-consuming part of learning the ancient craft of blacksmithing is learning how to build and maintain your coal forge fire. Unless you have an endless supply of coal, care must be taken early on to prevent the wasteful burning of your fuel. All blacksmiths have special tricks to help them light a fire. In time, you will learn what works best with your specific forge and coal supply.

A clean, concentrated hot flame is necessary for forging. It is very important to dispose of any clinkers as well as any leftover ash, cinders, and slag remaining in the fire pot and fire bed. Once clinkers have cooled, they are almost metallic in appearance and are very hard. A screen sifter may be used to separate these materials from the coke. Coke will also build up on the sides of the fire pot and fire bed, so it is important to remove any loose pieces that may have accumulated.

When setting up your fire, make sure that the tuyere at the bottom of the fire bed is closed. Before you begin, you can set up either one or two piles in the fire bed: a coal pile or a coal and a coke pile. These fuels will be raked or shoveled into the fire as it ignites and grows into a full flame.

Now that your forge is ready, it's time to light the fire. When you light your forge, you can use either coal or a combination of coal and coke. The following directions include the use of coal, but coke is easier to ignite than coal.

THE NEST

I start off with two full sheets of newspaper, tear them in half, and crumple them up into "eggs" or tight wads. Do not roll them or fold them—the more wrinkles and air pockets each ball has, the better.

1. Crumple sheets of newspaper into egg size balls for the center of your nest.

2, 3, 4. Place the eggs into the center of another full sheet of newspaper, sprinkle some fine coal dust into the pile, and fold all four corners into the center. Coal dust is the fine, black, powdery grain found in the bottom of the coal bag or can. You can also make dust by simply breaking a piece of coal into pieces. Place this upside down into another newspaper sheet and make a divot in the center creating a nest. Crunch the exposed edges up towards the center.

5, 6. Fold the bottom full sheet of newspaper with the eggs and coal dust inside, turning the nest upside down, and making a divot with your fist.

7. Light the crumpled edges of your nest and place it into the fire pot, making sure that the lit part is underneath, by the airflow.

8. Light the under side of the nest. In the background you can see lit newspaper heating the air in chimney, which will help start the upward draft.

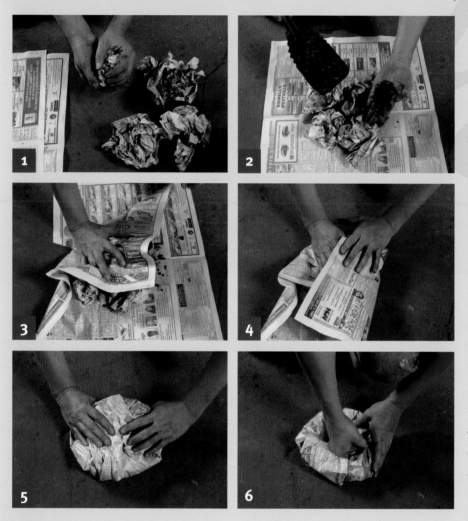

Trick of the Trade
Before lighting your nest, make sure that the air into the draft or chimney has been warmed. Burn a crumpled sheet of newspaper into the air intake to start the updraft.

Turn on the air or start cranking the squirrel cage to get enough airflow to ignite the paper nest. Sprinkle more coal dust and little pieces of coal from your fire bed into the nest and around its edges.

Once white or yellow smoke appears, add a bit more airflow and more coal. Continue this process, without disturbing the original hot spot where the nest is located.

9. Add coke or coal to the top of the nest and increase the airflow through the tuyere.

After you have created a steady stream of smoke and enough coal is glowing on the bottom, use your straight poker to open up the mound and release more air. Stick the poker into the lower center of the fire pot and lift the mound just enough to increase the airflow. This action will immediately reduce the amount of smoke generated and will allow the fire to produce the greatest amount of heat.

Continue to add coal slowly, waiting for the flames to rise out of the pile with each additional shovel. At this stage, you can increase the blower to help fuel the fire. Within a few minutes, a red glow should be visible at the bottom of the fire.

The process of adding coal, tapping down the top of the mound, and poking the center of the mound is repeated throughout your entire day of forging. These actions may initially seem high maintenance, but they will become second nature with experience. Make sure you have an established bed of hot coals before adding more fuel. Then you can start raking coal into and around the edge of the fire pot. To help burn the coal most efficiently, lightly sprinkle water on the coal before adding it to the fire. Continue adding coal and using the blower until you have amassed about four inches of flaming coal above and around the bed.

Trick of the Trade

One of the most common mistakes that occurs when lighting a coal forge is to pick and poke at it before it has had a chance to establish a good base. The second most common mistake is to over-pile the coal into a freshly ignited flame. The weight stops the airflow, which prevents the coal from catching fire.

Cross-section of a banked fire.

The center of your fire comprises coal that has been converted into clean-burning coke. The greenish-yellow smoke is being generated from the outside perimeter of green coal that is igniting and burning. In order to control the smoke, use your poker and make an opening near the side and top of the flame mound—this will allow for the flames from the core of the coal pile to escape. Breaking up this "shell" of not quite burnt coal will allow more oxygen to penetrate and escape—causing a hotter fire. When tending your fire, always work from the outside to the inside, bringing the green coal to the center of your fire.

Banking a fire is the process of setting up the burning coal with a thick layer of moist green coal on top of an already heated mound and then shutting off the blower. This will keep the coal burning slowly for several hours if done properly and allows the smith to work away from the forge without having to rebuild a fire. At the end of the day, the coal fire should not be banked, but pulled apart and left to burn out. Shutting down your coal forge will be discussed at the end of this chapter.

As a beginner blacksmith, it is easier and cheaper to maintain a small fire. Your fire size should be no less than the size of softball, but a larger fire can be created if necessary for the task. The majority of projects in this book suggest using stock sizes of 1/4 to 1/2 inch (0.5 to 1 cm) diameter—a softball size fire mound should work quite well.

CROSS SECTION OF A BANKED FIRE

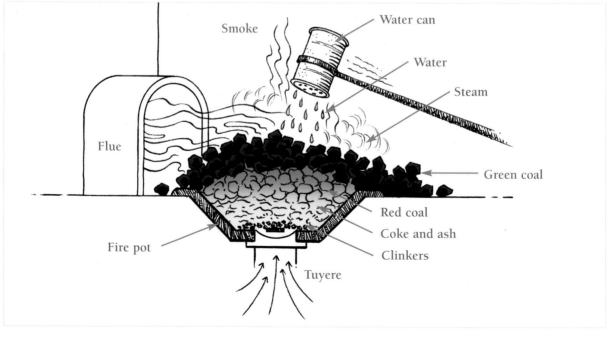

Working with Tongs

It is essential that you are able to hold your heated metal stock securely when working at your forge and anvil. Although you may be able to hold your material with a gloved hand, more often than not, you will need to use a pair of tongs. As discussed earlier, tongs are available in all sorts of shapes and sizes. The two main styles you will use will hold flat stock or square or round stock.

If the reins of the tongs are open too far for you hand to grip securely, then the tongs are too small. When you have a proper fit of material size and shape, you will have greater success with each hammer blow as you move the metal the way you want it.

When gripping the stock that you will place in the fire, make sure that the jaws of the tongs close evenly on the iron piece. Proper tongs will hold the material securely and evenly. If the stock shifts within the jaws of the tongs, then the tongs are too big.

A tong ring or clip can be placed over the reins of the tongs to help ensure that the stock remains firmly locked in the tongs. This will help hold the tong reins together, allowing you to loosen up on your grip.

The tongs on the left fit the material better than the tongs on the right. Notice the handle spread.

This image shows the proper positioning of flat stock.

Here, the jaws of the tongs that do not sufficiently wrap around the bar stock, therefore the stock will pivot when you are striking it. This is dangerous and inefficient.

An adjustable tong clip may be used to secure the handles.

How to Heat Your Iron Stock

Because iron is not a good conductor of heat, the material provides several advantages to the blacksmith. One end of a piece of bar stock can be heated to forging temperature while the opposite end will stay relatively cool. Because of its low conductivity, a heated section of bar stock is also slow to lose its temperature. Be aware that even if a piece of stock has not begun changing color while in the forge, the metal is still very hot.

When placing your material into the forge, it is important to keep the stock horizontal and to place it in the center of your hot coals, in the area where the coke is being produced. Position the stock so it is lying on the coals, not in the coals. If you submerge the stock into the coals you will likely end up losing sight of the stock and be unable to see the color changes as the metal temperature increases. All sides of your stock should be heated evenly, and it may be necessary to rotate the stock while it is in the forge. Remember to maintain this visual; otherwise you will significantly increase the risk of overheating or burning the metal.

When stock becomes heated and remains at a high temperature, a scaly surface forms. This is called fire scale, and it is a natural occurrence when forging mild steel. All metal naturally oxidizes, but an increase in temperature accelerates the rate of oxidation. Fire scale is dangerous because it will spring off of your hot metal stock as you make impact with your hammer. These flakes of fire scale will expose you to the possibility of skin burns.

Use a stiff bristled brush on your heated metal stock before striking. Not only will this greatly reduce the amount of hot airborne fire scale flakes, but it also reduces the amount of fire scale on the metal stock. If fire scale is left unattended on the materials, it will become embedded into the stock when you hammer, resulting in a permanently pitted surface.

Trick of the Trade

Because all basic forging techniques can be performed at a bright orange heat, I would recommend that beginner blacksmiths use this color as their indicator, rather than the higher temperature yellow heat. This will reduce the possibility of burning your stock and will also help limit the amount of oxidation which leads to fire scale.

Always place stock into the forge horizontally.

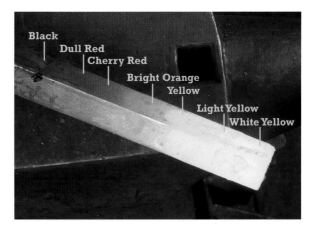

Black
Dull Red
Cherry Red
Bright Orange
Yellow
Light Yellow
White Yellow

Forging is most effective when the metal has turned yellow.

Temperature Color Indication

The most common way for blacksmiths to determine when their metal stock has reached the correct forging temperature is by the change in color that occurs when the iron is in the forge. Through trial and error, you will be able to distinguish these color patterns.

Bending can occur when the stock appears red in color (approximately 1400°F, 760°C). All other basic forging techniques can be performed at a bright orange color (approximately 1800°F, 982°C), but forging is most effective when the metal has a yellow appearance (approximately 2100°F, 1149°C). Forge welding mild steel requires a light yellow (2300°F, 1260°C) heat and there is an entire chapter in this book dedicated to forge welding techniques. If your stock takes on a whitish appearance, you have started the process of burning your material. Mild steel burns at 2400°F (1316°C).

—⟫—

Burns—The first time hurts… The second time still hurts, but you kind of expected it since you're playing with fire. The third time still hurts, but you've accepted it as a souvenir. The fourth time hurts less; consider it tough love. The fifth time…. yes, there will be a fifth time.

—⟫—

Once you have removed a heated piece of iron from the forge, do not set it on the face of the anvil until

Selecting a Forging Hammer

The size and shape of your forging hammer is dependent on the size of the stock you are forging as well as your personal size and shape. Unless you are trying to forge a large mass of metal, brute force is not as important as accurate and controlled hammer blows.

I have seen many beginners start out with hammers that are simply too heavy for them. When I started smithing, I used a 2½ pound (1.1 kg) cross peen hammer. Today, I do the majority of my forging with a slightly smaller hammer—1½ pounds (0.7 kg). This allows me to be at my anvil for many hours without tiring. Listen to your body in order to determine if the weight of your hammer needs to change.

If you are maintaining a correct posture and striking motion but your wrists are sore, increase the weight of the hammer a little. When the hammer is too light for the work, your wrist will have a tendency to push into the heated material, rather then letting the force of the hammer blow move the metal. If you tire after a short while, decrease the weight of the hammer.

> ## Trick of the Trade
> Keep two different-sized cross peen hammers available. Switch out as your body and the materials dictate.

PROPER STANCE AND HAMMER SWING

Forging iron is a physically demanding process because you are working in a contained area with an open fire, hot metal, and a hammer and tongs in hand. It is important to stay alert and focused, and to maintain good posture while keeping your hands, body, and feet in a relaxed state.

Using the tongs held in your passive hand, remove the heated stock from the forge. With your dominant hand, maintain a firm grip on your hammer, but do not over-grip. Over-gripping means having such a tight hold on the hammer handle that your hand will lock into that position. Prolonged over-gripping can result in serious wrist or tendon wear. Your grip should be tight enough so that the hammer does not leave you, but also loose enough that you can rotate the hammer from face to ping simply by letting it swing inside of your grip.

—⁄⁄⁄—

I have a tendency to grip the hammer higher up the handle than most blacksmiths. I probably got used to that position, and it is the most comfortable for me. It could also be that what I concentrate on now, as an artist and blacksmith, is smaller in scale and force.

—⁄⁄⁄—

The best method to find the most comfortable hammer grip is to hold your arm out horizontally in from of you. The comfort of that position will determine if you need to raise or lower your hand position up or down the handle. What feels the best with your arm extended usually is the best grip when forging.

Correct posture when forging is vital for healthy lower-back and shoulder muscles. When approaching your anvil, stand up straight while maintaining a slight bend at the waist. This stance provides the best balance for full force hammering. Reposition yourself around the anvil so that you can adequately reach the desired work surface of your metal. If you do not move your body and merely try to lean over the anvil, your lower back muscles will sound alarm bells shortly into the process.

When preparing to strike the metal, your hammer arm shoulder should be positioned almost directly above the desired point of contact. Your goal is to control the hammer swing using your arm muscles, not your wrist. Using your shoulders, as well as your elbows, keeps pressure off your wrist.

The force of your hammer swing will depend upon how far you raise your arm from the work surface. Because you are working with tools in both hands, the

The forging hammer has a wide cross peen and a large, slightly domed face. Some smiths prefer the cross peen to be lower than the center to help them see the piece they are forging.

probability of smashing your thumb with your hammer is very low. When starting out, try to maintain a consistent hammer swing, raising the hammer to your chest level between strikes.

When striking with a swinging arm motion, do not arch up or attempt to use your lower back muscles when raising the hammer between blows. As a beginner, you are using muscles to perform actions that they may have never experienced before.

Similar to any physical activity, it will take a bit of time and repetitive practice to build up your stamina and endurance. Pain or tightness in your muscles is the first sign that your posture needs to change, the weight of your hammer needs to be lightened, or that you simply need to stop and take a break.

Trick of the Trade

Hammering exercises will help improve your motor skills. I suggest getting pieces of 2 x 4 inch (5 x 10 cm) wood, a carpenter's hammer, and bag of #10 nails. Every day, a week or two before you begin forging for the first time, hammer a dozen nails into the wood.

Proper posture will keep you smithing for years to come.

THE NEAR AND FAR SIDE

The following images show the different placement of hammer blows to stock and stock placement on the anvil. Each placement has a specific name and these terms are used throughout the exercises.

1

Full Face Parallel

2

Full Face Angle

3

Half Face Near

4

Half Face Far

5

Anvil Edge Near

6

Anvil Edge Far

7

Back Face

HOW TO USE YOUR ANVIL

Face—This is the most commonly used section of an anvil and it is used for a variety of purposes such as welding, drawing, and upsetting.

Table—This serves a similar function as the face, but offers an alternative surface for cutting stock with a chisel.

Horn—Used to make scrolls and curves as well as drawing.

Edge—A straight edge can be used for making bends that are 90 degrees or less. Either through design or by use, the edge may be rounded and this makes a good area for starting a scroll.

Heel—Used to bend stock when the desired angle is 90 degrees or more.

Drop—Used for bending stock.

Pritchel (round hole located on face)—Used for punching holes.

Hardy (square hole located on face)—Used to hold various anvil tools.

How to Shut Down Your Coal Forge

In order to prevent wasting fuel, once you are finished forging for the day, simply rake away the unburned coal on the perimeter of your fire and scrape out the coke that has accumulated on the sides of your fire pot. This will speed up the time needed for the fire to burn out. The next time you light the forge, you will have some coke to begin the fire. Be sure to clean out those nasty clinkers before starting your next fire.

—m—

When I first started to learn about blacksmithing, I received a lot of information from blacksmiths who freely shared their knowledge. Make the effort to attend any conferences or workshops located in your neck of the woods. There are a lot of experienced metalworkers out there who are willing to share their knowledge and insight with you.

—m—

2 Getting Your Hands Dirty

Now that you have an understanding of the tools and materials, it's time to bang some metal. We are going to cover the universal skills and techniques used by all blacksmiths and learn how to make useful, yet beautiful items for your home and garden.

CHAPTER FIVE

TOOL USAGE AND FORGING TECHNIQUES

This book is for the person who has always wanted to try blacksmithing, but has never had the opportunity. It is my desire to present the basic tool usage and forging techniques in the simplest manner possible. As you become more knowledgeable of the terminology, tools, and procedures, there will be more resource material for you to grow with.

Trick of the Trade

Although it is important for you to become accustomed with the use of tongs, I would like to suggest that your initial practice exercises incorporate longer parent stock material. The additional stock length will eliminate the need for tongs. When you have become comfortable with all of the steps in the forging processes, then tongs can be introduced.

How to Use Anvil Tools

All of these tools can be used without the assistance of a striker, but you will need a portable leg stand or a hold down tool to help keep the stock in position for some of these techniques.

HOT CUT OR HARDY CHISEL

You can use a marking tool to designate the desired cutoff point, or you can decide visually. Insert the hot cut into the hardy hole of the anvil. Heat your stock to a bright orange color temperature and place it on the hardy chisel at the cutoff point.

Find a solid copper or brass mallet for all of your hot cutting. These metals are softer than iron and will help preserve the sharp edge of your hardy chisel, should you accidentally hit the tool with your hammer while cutting.

There are two ways to hot cut stock. Remember that it is important to use vertical hammer blows when performing this task:

1. **Rotating**—This procedure gives the cut ends a nice clean edge. Although it may be a bit difficult to perform at first, it produces a nice, clean, cutoff. Insert your hot cut into the hardy hole of the anvil. Place the heated orange temperature color section of stock on the cutting edge of the hardy. Use medium blows to notch the surface of the stock that comes in direct contact with the hardy edge. Rotate the stock and continue to hammer as you create a notched line around the circumference. Repeat this process until the notched area is almost completely through the width of the stock material. Lighten up your hammer blows when nearing the center of the stock, and break the stock into two pieces.

2. **Stationary**—This type of hot cut holds the designated cutoff over the chisel and hammer. Between strikes, look for a dark line to appear on the stock's contact surface. Once this line becomes visible, stop making direct hammer blows above the chisel edge.

There are three ways to separate the cut end of the stock from the parent stock:

1. Use a pair of tongs to grab the cut end and bend it back and forth to break the pieces apart.

2. Insert the cut end of the stock into the pritchel hole and use your hand grip to bend or break off the parent section.

3. Lay the parent stock on the face of the anvil with the notched hot cut lined up on the far edge of the anvil face. Hammer the cut end downwards until the piece breaks off.

Safety Tip

Overly forceful hammer blows are unproductive and unsafe. Direct contact between your hammer face and the chisel edge will not only result in a dulled cutting edge, but the chance of hot metal flying through the air is significantly increased. Your goal is to successfully cut the stock into two pieces—not perform the task in less than ten seconds flat.

COLD CUT

Insert the cold cut into the hardy hole and place your stock material so that the chisel edge is aligned with the desired cutoff point.

Follow the same rotating procedure as the hot cut, except your objective is to nick and score the entire circumference of the stock with direct heavy hammer. Be sure to lighten up on the hammer blows before cutting completely through. Cold cuts can be sheared off or bent back and forth until the stock is broken into two sections.

—⚍—

Cold cutting metal stock is more intense than hot cutting. Use a piece of 1/4 inch (0.5 cm) stock material to practice this exercise and you will learn how laborious it can be. Fortunately, I have a chop saw that I use to cut my stock materials. Although it is a practical task worth knowing, cold cutting requires a lot of effort for such a simple task.

—⚍—

FULLER/SWAGE

The key to forging an even fuller is to make sure you keep your stock parallel to the fuller edges. If the stock is angled, it will show up in the material's fullered or pinched area—usually in the form of an angled or pinched mark. To ensure that the indentations are forged equally, keep your stock parallel to the face of the anvil.

BOTTOM FULLER

For this exercise, use a 20 inch (51 cm) length of 3/8 inch (1 cm) round or square stock. Heat that portion of the stock you will be shaping to a bright orange temperature color.

While the stock is heating, insert the square shank of the bottom fuller into the hardy hole. The length of the fuller should be parallel with the long edges of your anvil.

Place the heated portion of the stock on the fuller's edge and strike down with direct medium blows. This

A fullered piece of bar stock.

will indent one area of the hot stock. This "pinching" can be made deeper with continued heating and hammering, and the area that is being fullered can continue around the perimeter of the stock—just rotate the stock while hammering.

FULLER SET

Since the top tool of a set is handled, fullering with sets requires an additional person. The secondary smith holds the top tool in place while the smith controls the stock and hammer.

SPRING FULLER

The top and bottom dies are connected with a spring. A striker, fly press, or mechanical hammer is needed to use this tool.

HARDY SPRING FULLER

The hardy spring fuller allows the smith to work alone. The top and bottom dies are connected with a spring and the bottom die has a square shank welded on for the hardy.

This spring fuller rests inside the hardy hole of the anvil.

Use a 20 inch (51 cm) length of 1 x ¼ inch (3 x 0.5 cm) rectangular stock and heat 2 to 3 inches (5 to 8 cm) of one end. Place the center of the heated portion inside the spring fuller edges and hammer with direct medium blows. Rotate the stock 90 degrees and even out any distortions in the midsection.

The instruction for using swage tooling is the same procedure used for fuller tools.

Tapering

Tapering or "drawing out" means to lengthen the stock material by reducing its original mass. Tapering is the most commonly used forging technique, and it is the first step in learning how to move hot metal.

Start out with 20 inches (51 cm) of ⅜ inch (1 cm) round stock. Place a 1 to 2 inch (3 to 5 cm) section of the bar stock into the fire. Make sure that the stock is resting horizontally in the forge and heat the end until it is bright orange in appearance.

Remove the stock from the fire. If any fire scale has appeared on the material's surface, quickly wire brush the scale away.

Use the face of the anvil as a table support for your first hammer blow. Start by squaring off the round stock and remember that every hammer blow you make will affect the opposing side.

—〰—

When teaching this procedure, I ask students to square-off just the tip of the stock at first. This way they will be assured of square edges before continuing with the rest of the taper.

—〰—

Your initial blows should be full face and flat on the anvil. They are not intended to draw out the material, but to establish the square. Hammer twice on the first surface, rotate 90 degrees, and hammer two times on this surface, keeping both blows at the tip of the material.

Verify that you have successfully squared-off the tip by looking at your material head-on. This is the time to correct any trapezoid shapes from over-hammering one side or not rotating a full 90 degrees to form the other two sides.

Reheat just 2 inches (5 cm) or so of the material. Remember to shut off the forge airflow before taking the stock out of the fire. This habit will save you lots of coal. While the stock is reheating, make sure to clear your anvil face of any loose fire scale and remember to perform a quick wire brushing on your stock after you remove it from the forge.

Now that the square surfaces have been established, you can use more force to move the metal. Place the heated tip on the farthest edge of the anvil face. Slightly raise the back end of the stock (the part you are holding), and slightly angle the hammer's face to match the angle of the stock. By keeping the stock and hammer in these positions, you will achieve a taper much quicker.

To understand this positioning (using the far edge of the anvil face), try tapering a piece of stock at the edge nearest you. With the hammer slightly angled, you will find that the hammer's edge makes contact with the anvil face before hitting the heated material.

Reheat when you lose the orange color (remember to place the stock material in the forge horizontally) and check the material for fire scale before continuing to forge. Remember to turn off the blower in between heats. All of the supporting side tasks that are performed when reheating will come naturally to you with patience and practice.

While overlapping, make a slightly angled blow from the base of the heated material to the tip, and draw out the metal. The longer the taper gets, the thinner the stock becomes, thus providing a graceful point at the end. Rotate 90 degrees, but it is not necessary to rotate to a full 360 degrees. A 90 degree back-and-forth turn of the wrist will suffice.

After you have drawn out the tip, your next step is to return it back to round. Breaking the corners you have made while tapering is easy.

Reheat the material, place it on the anvil face directly on the corner edge, and hammer the opposing edge. Reheat and rotate 90 degrees and break the corners of the other two sides. This will give your taper a faceted hexagon shape.

Reheat for the final rounding off process, which requires a slow rolling of the stock back and forth, with quick planishing hammer strokes. Planishing is hammering that smoothes out the surface ridges that were created during the forging process. It requires quick and light hammer blows and should not be performed if the metal stock is heated higher than a cherry red heat. Be sure that when the face of your hammer comes into contact with the face of the stock, the two faces are parallel.

Congratulations, you have just forged your first piece of metal. Hot cut the tapered portion off and do another one. If you are having difficulty in the squaring up of round stock process, cut to the chase and use 3/8 inch (1 cm) –square stock. This short cut helps beginners because the 90 degree wrist turns are already established for you. After you are comfortable tapering square stock, you can return to tapering round stock.

The tapering of square stock follows the same process as round stock, but you do not have to break the corners and round them off. Square stock tapers have a totally different look to them that works well with the added embellishment of twisting.

As you continue to practice tapering, simply hot cut the tapers off your stock material and make another one. Doing this one activity several times in a row will help you establish a forging habit. Once you have familiarized yourself with the drawing out process, you can begin changing the length of your tapers and also experiment using different stock sizes.

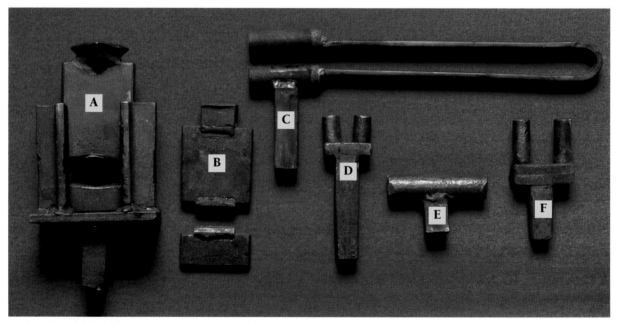

Hardy tools: guillotine (A), auxiliary dies for guillotine (B), spring fuller (C), bending fork (D), roll bar (E), and large bending fork (F).

Be sure and save your tapered tips. Lay them out and be encouraged by the progression of your skills. I still have a jar of my first tapers chronicling how long, difficult, and rewarding the learning process was.

—◆◆◆—

Spreading

This forging technique reduces the thickness of material stock while increasing its width. It is best achieved by using the face and cross peen of your hammer. Spreading is most commonly used in forging fishtail scrolls, but it is also used in creating leaf shapes.

Start out with a 20 inch (51 cm) length of 3/8-inch (1 cm) -round stock. Heat 1 inch (3 cm) of the end to a bright orange color temperature and lay the heated stock on the face of the anvil.

Using medium, head-on blows, flatten one side of your stock using your hammer's face. Carry the flattened surface farther down the stock while gradually lightening-up on your hammer blows. Your objective is to create a graceful transition from the round stock material to its flattened end.

Reheat the flattened end and return it to the anvil. Rotate your hammer grip 180 degrees so that the cross peen will make contact with your hot metal stock. Start to hammer—the cross peen's marks should create a series of dimples that radiate outward. This is done

HOW TO SPREAD THE TIP OF STEEL WITH THE HAMMER'S CROSS PEEN

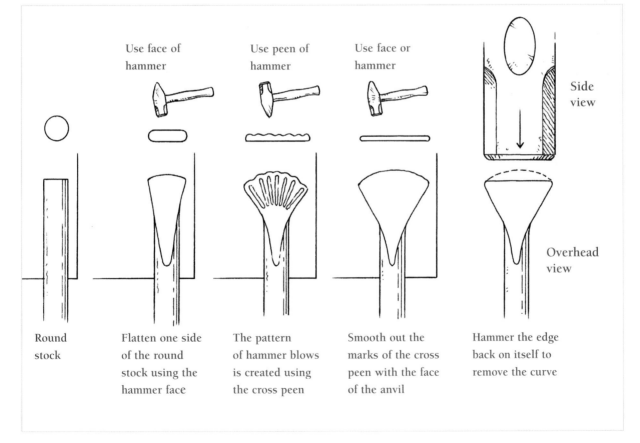

Use face of hammer

Use peen of hammer

Use face or hammer

Side view

Overhead view

Round stock

Flatten one side of the round stock using the hammer face

The pattern of hammer blows is created using the cross peen

Smooth out the marks of the cross peen with the face of the anvil

Hammer the edge back on itself to remove the curve

TOOL USAGE AND FORGING TECHNIQUES

71

Rotate your hammer angle and stock angle to spread the tip of your metal stock.

The trick to a good upset is to concentrate the heat just in the small area you wish to compress. If the heat is longer then the thickness of the stock, there is a tendency to bend the stock rather than compress it. It is vital that you use heavy blows when upsetting metal—light blows will only flatten the edges, not compress them.

Start by heating the very tip (1/2 inch [1 cm] or less) of a 12-inch (30 cm) -long piece of 3/8-inch (1 cm) -round or square stock. If the heat is longer than that, quickly pour a stream of water on the backside of the heated material to cool off the excess and concentrate the heat.

Place the heated tip of the stock just past the far side of the anvil and using horizontal or backing up blows, hammer directly onto the tip's surface. Rotate the stock continuously while hammering to prevent any bending.

Some anvils have upsetting blocks located just below the anvil face. To use this area, place the heated stock against the block, and using both arms, pound the yellow hot tip into the block. This method is good for larger, heavier stock sizes. The weight of the bar and the action of your body bringing it down upon itself will expand the heated tip. You can also put an anvil on the floor to upset longer pieces of heavy stock.

If your anvil does not have a low block on its base, but the stock length is short enough (12 inches [30 cm] or less), one person can easily upset the tip of the stock by placing the heated portion directly on-end, on the face of the anvil. Use hammer blows on the cold, upright end to compress and upset the heated tip.

Proper upsetting requires a clean and level end on your stock material. Make sure that the tip to be upset is smooth and even. After each heat, straighten out any uneven curves that have occurred—do all straightening before you reheat the tip.

by rotating your hammer angle and the stock's angle on the anvil face. The width of the material will begin to spread outward.

Rotate your hammer grip and use the face of the hammer to smooth out the ridges of the cross peen. Reheat if necessary to complete this task.

Upsetting

Although learning new things can be frustrating, upsetting metal means something entirely different. Upsetting is a means of compressing a mass of metal to be larger than the original stock size. It allows you to increase the thickness of stock material at any given point. This technique is used to make items such as nail heads, spoons, or decorative ends on stock tips. It is also the initial step in scarfing steel—a technique that needs to be learned in order to forge weld, which will be discussed in the next chapter of this book.

As you are preparing to upset, remember that the cold anvil surface will accelerate the cooling off of heated materials.

Make sure to rotate the stock material with every blow to ensure an even mass build-up on the tip.

Bending

Heated metal can be bent into numerous shapes, from flowing curves to sharp 90 degree angles. The trick to bending curves is to start off with and maintain an even heat. Bending does not require the same color temperature heat as forging—an orange heat will allow you to bend the stock.

Stock material can be bent using several methods:

1. The stock can be placed over the horn or face of the anvil and hammered down.

2. The stock can be placed in the hardy bending fork and bent using a handheld bending fork.

3. The stock can be secured in the vise jaws and bent or wrapped around another piece of material.

4. If you heat the center section of a piece of stock, use tongs to grip the ends of the material and manually bend the length of metal.

The key to successful bending is the length and evenness of your heat. Remember that metal will bend the easiest where it is the hottest.

MAKING A 90 DEGREE ANGLE BEND

The area of your stock that will have the bend will be subjected to a series of hammer blows. If that area is not built-up with the upsetting process, the bend will be thinner than the rest of the stock.

Take a 15 inch (38 cm) length of ½ inch (1 cm) -square stock and heat a small section, about 3 inches (8 cm) from the tip, to an orange color temperature.

Trick of the Trade
Try and keep the heat centralized to the area that is to be bent. Heating up longer sections will result in avoidable distortions. You can quench and quickly cool off sections that have taken too much heat before hammering.

TIPS FOR FORGING A 90 DEGREE ANGLE BEND

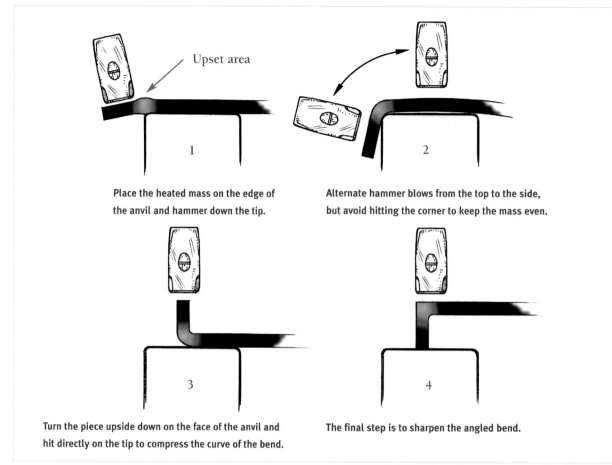

1

Place the heated mass on the edge of the anvil and hammer down the tip.

2

Alternate hammer blows from the top to the side, but avoid hitting the corner to keep the mass even.

3

Turn the piece upside down on the face of the anvil and hit directly on the tip to compress the curve of the bend.

4

The final step is to sharpen the angled bend.

Place one end of the stock on the anvil face and hammer down the other end. This will swell up the small portion of the stock where the bend will occur.

Place the stock on the anvil face so that the upset area is resting on the edge of the anvil (see figure 1). The first hammer blows should occur off the edge of the anvil. In addition to creating the intentional bend, the stock length that is resting on the anvil will have a tendency to bend as well. Correct this by alternating hammer blows to this area. Avoid any direct hammer blows on the upset area until finishing the 90 degree bend.

Never hit the corner of the stock when trying to make a 90 degree bend. This would result in an angled, faceted corner, or the upset area will be thinner than the rest of the stock length.

When practicing 90 degree bends, you will find that the least amount of hammer blows results in the nicest bend. The inside corner of the bend will be shaped by the anvil surface, so you do not need to directly hammer on the inside angles. All of your hammer blows should make contact with the outside of the bend.

BENDING A FLAT BAR ON ITS EDGE

Whether you are trying to bend a piece of flat bar at a 90 degree angle or just a gradual radius, the important thing to remember is the reaction of the metal. The outer edge of the flat stock will increase in length, while the inside edge compresses. To avoid a thin outer edge, hammer blows connecting with the compressed side should follow through and spread to the outside. The sharper the curve, the more distortion will occur.

Take a 15 inch (38 cm) length of 1" by ¼" (2.5 x 0.5 cm) flat bar and heat a long section of the tip, about 6 inches (15 cm), to an orange color temperature. You will need to use tongs for this exercise—the tongs should securely hold the flat stock by its edges, not by its width.

Place the heated portion, edge up, on the soft radius of the far side of the anvil or the horn, and hammer the tip downward.

You should notice that the metal wants to bend where there is the least amount of resistance—on the width planes. Alternating your hammer blows from the edge to the face of the stock will help keep distortions from getting out of hand.

Sharper bends require a smaller length of orange heat. As the flat stock begins to bend, try to avoid any direct hammer blows on the outer edges of the stock material. When you alternate blows to the face of the stock, you will need to flatten outward the compressed area that accumulates on the inside of the bend.

Scrolling

Scrolling is probably the most recognizable motif in blacksmithing. Its beauty lies in its simplicity and the countless symmetrical variations found in traditional ironwork such as gates, railings, and fences. Scrolls can be made of round stock, square stock, or even rectangular flat bar stock. Bending is the initial step for scrolling and a good scroll will take several heats to accomplish.

You will have a better sense of the proportions and scroll curves if you concentrate on the negative space created in the spiral center. Your objective is to have that space increase gradually as the iron spiral opens up. Work slowly, and if it will help you to have a visual reference, draw a chalk spiral on your floor or layout table to serve as a guide. If the scroll gets out of whack, and you find yourself spending more than a few minutes trying to correct it, toss it on the floor and start over again. Save your time and energy for the actual learning process. Once you are more familiar

Scrolls always start from the inside, which is where the curves will be the tightest. Care must be taken when bending the scroll tip before continuing with the scroll.

with scrolling, you will be able to perform corrective measures much easier.

—〰—

There are three basic scroll shapes: the single or spiral, the S shape, and the C shape. Numerous combinations of these forms allow for a limitless number of patterns. When I forge the elements for a job requiring scroll-work, I lay out the scrolls in different patterns and photograph the designs for future reference before assembling the elements.

—〰—

STOCK LENGTH

You may be surprised at the length of a piece of material needed to make a scroll. Using chalk, draw a scroll on your floor or on your worktable. Using a cloth tape measure, follow the curves and measure the total length of your scroll. You will see that it takes approximately 24 inches (61 cm) of stock to create a 6 inch (15 cm) diameter spiral.

DRESSING THE SCROLL TIP

A finished tip on a scroll is the foremost indicator that a metal scroll was handmade and not machine bent. Make an effort to dress the tips of your scrolls, even for practice exercises.

Square taper—the basic drawing out on all four sides of a point.

Round taper—same as a square taper, but with no corner edges.

Square ribbon taper—the material is tapered down to a graceful end on one set of opposing sides. The other two sides retain the width of the original stock size.

Fish tail—the cross peen side of the hammer and strike down the tip of your material into a radius pattern—this will make the tip wider than the remaining length of stock.

Snub end—this tip incorporates the smooth transition of a ribbon taper ending in a cylindrical mass.

Upset one $^1/_2$ inch (1 cm) tip of the stock material. When enough mass has been formed, place the stock horizontally on the anvil so that the upset mass extends past the far edge of the anvil. Use backing blows to shape the upset mass, but use your tapering skills to maintain the width of the remaining stock length. Remember to use your passive hand grip to raise and lower the stock—this will help you in rounding the tip. Gently hammer the tip back onto the tapered portion of your material to make a slight curved crease.

Hey penny—this scroll tip is a tapered flat bar that ends with a disc or coined shape at the end.

Use the face of the anvil to round the edges of your flat stock. Then, with the flattened end extended over the far edge of the anvil, use one-sided hammer blows on the stock resting on the anvil face.

FORGING A SCROLL

You can use the soft radius edge of the far side of the anvil or the horn to initiate the first curve. Begin the curve by placing the heated tip slightly past the edge of the horn and use light hammer blows, striking downward. Keep your stock horizontal and flat on the anvil face as you hammer over the edge of the scroll tip.

Once this curve has been created, turn the stock over and place the curved portion on the anvil face and lightly apply back blow hammering. As you are hammering toward you, use your passive grip arm to move the stock in an up and down fashion off the anvil face. Remember that you will heat different sections of the stock material as you complete the curve.

Trick of the Trade
If a scroll develops a flat area, the best way to correct it is to heat the area, place it in the hardy fork, and using a handheld bending fork, tweak the area that is flat.

Continually repeat this sequence, using blows that only hit the material. Just keep hitting the scroll with light hammer back blows in a radius pattern, until the material turns on top of itself and creates a graceful scroll.

COMMON SCROLL TIPS

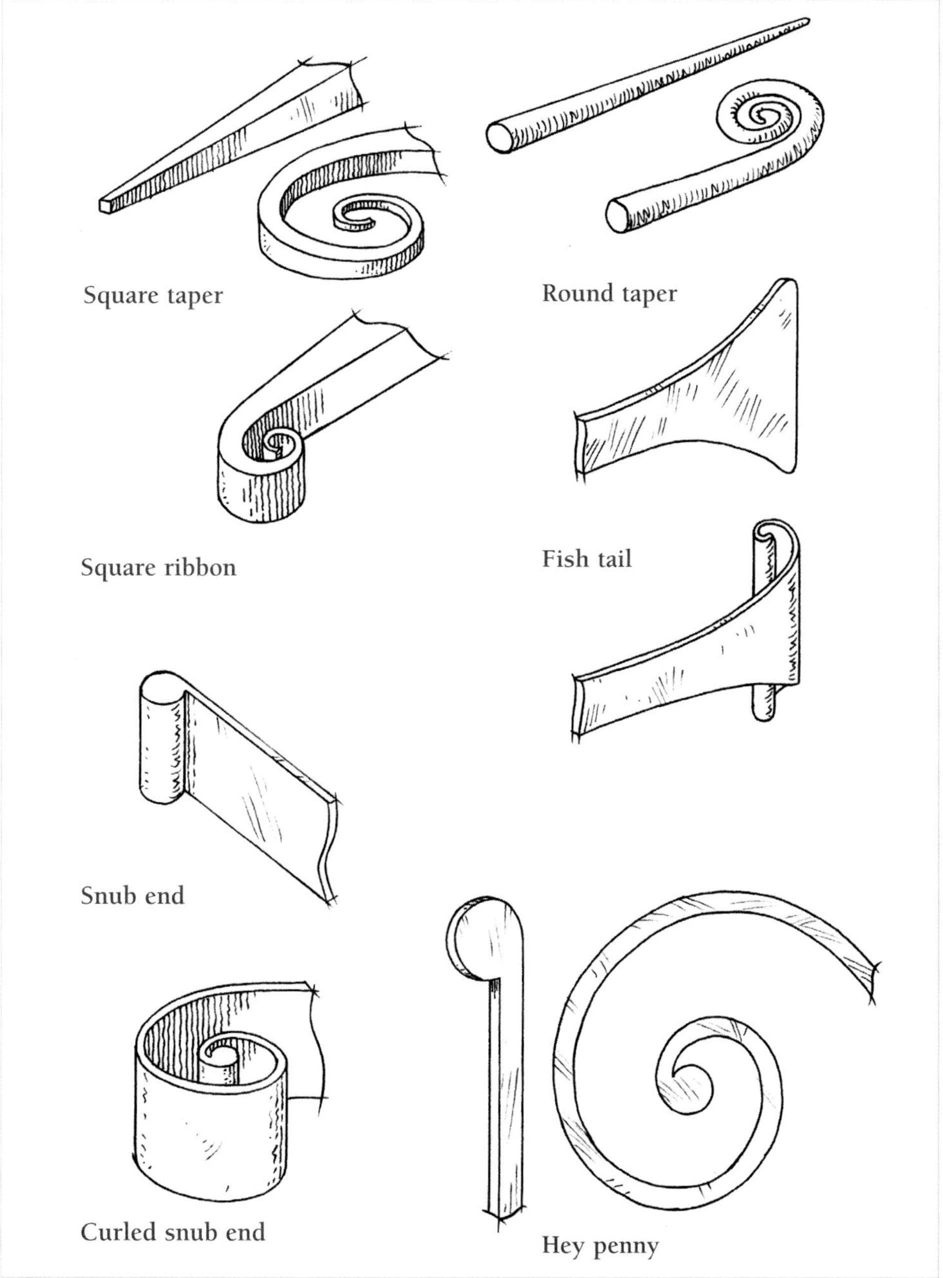

Square taper

Round taper

Square ribbon

Fish tail

Snub end

Curled snub end

Hey penny

When you need to make many scrolls that are exactly the same, make yourself a jig. Scroll jigs are formed the same way that scrolls are, except they are not flat and they are made with thicker material to accommodate the heat and pressure of repetitive forming. The jig not only spirals out, it also has a raised center to allow the material you are scrolling an easier access point. Form the jig's starting point with a fishtail scroll. This scroll needs to have a flat side, so after the spreading is finished, hammer down past the taper to raise the fishtail up and create a level bottom.

Continue with the scroll process making sure that the flat side remains flush with the anvil face.

Weld this jig onto a piece of angle iron so that it can be secured into the jaws of the leg vise. I have some jigs that fit into the hardy hole of my anvil but they are small and do not require anything past a half revolution. For jigs that will require you to walk around as you feed the stock material in, it is better to use a stationary leg vise.

Initial formation of a scroll using a jig

Trick of the Trade

Once you make a jig you can always use it to make smaller scrolls. Just measure the length of the smaller scroll and mark it on the jig. When feeding the material in, stop at the designated point.

I like to use a pair of vise grips to hold the back end of the material as I walk around the jig and form the scroll. I first

Completing formation of a scroll using a jig

Removing a scroll from a jig

Trick of the Trade

One of the drawbacks to the coal forge is that the fire pot size regulates how long of a heat your stock material can achieve. When scrolling on large jigs, you will need to do the process in steps. The jigs raised center makes the scroll raised as well. Flattening the scroll you make should occur only after all of the wrapping has occurred.

take a grinder to the jaws of the vise grip and remove the teeth. The pressure of the grip still holds the material but the end does not get marred in the process.

To flatten the formed scroll, just place it on the anvil face with the center pointing up and tap down. If this is done with ample heat left over from the wrap, then there is not need to reheat.

 Safety Tip

Be aware that the jig will become very hot after only a few scrolls.

Another method is to use the hardy bending form to shape the scroll. This technique has an advantage because you can see the shape being formed face on. The negative space of the curl or scroll is just as important as the metal itself, and seeing that space develop as the iron curls will help you greatly. The bending fork will leave little marks from the contact points on the stock, but they are located on the inside and outside of the curls, not the front and back, which are the most visible sides of the scroll.

Upset the end of the stock to initiate a snub end scroll tip.

Start the scrolling process with the tip located off the far edge of the anvil.

For this exercise, use a 20 inch (51 cm) length of 1" x $\frac{1}{4}$" (3 x 0.5 cm) diameter flat bar. Heat the tip and dress it. I chose a snub end, but feel free to dress the tip however you would like. Even for practice exercises, make the effort to dress the tip of your material.

Reheat the stock and use the soft radius of the far edge of the anvil to curve the first $\frac{1}{2}$ inch (1 cm) of stock. Compress the tip by hammering directly down upon it.

Reheat and bring the stock to rest past the anvil edge and lightly hammer the stock in air, meaning, you should not use the anvil surface for resistance. This will allow you to make a graceful curve with the least amount of flat edges.

Rotate the material 180 degrees and place the curved portion up. Hammer, using back blows and light downward blows. Changing the angle of your tong arm will improve the accuracy of your hammer blows, creating a more graceful curve.

This process is continued with sections of the spiral being heated and shaped as you work down the length of stock. As the spiral increases in size, you will want to use the hardy bending fork and handheld bending fork.

Rotate the stock and use back blows to initiate the curl.

MAKE AN S SCROLL

Use an 8-inch (20 cm) length of ⅜ x ¼ inch (1 x 0.5 cm) stock. Ribbon dress both ends. On the second side, start your curve on the soft edge of the anvil face. Carry through similar to the spiral shape for 1 ¼ revolutions. Gauge the spiral by using the tip of the scroll as a guide or starting point to show a full 360 degrees and beyond.

Place the other finished end of the stock in the forge, heat, and repeat this initial process.

Make sure that the first scroll is facing up when you begin the second scroll. If it is facing downward, you end up with a C Scroll. While this isn't necessarily a bad thing, try to finish through with an S scroll before attempting an unintentional C scroll.

—⧟—

I have a hard time remembering which direction the scroll tip should be facing when making S and C scrolls. My mentor, Elmer Roush, told me just to remember the phrase "heads up" when creating an S scroll. This simple phrase has allowed me to quickly access whether I am about to form and S or C scroll.

—⧟—

This exercise can be repeated using stock of any length or size. This same procedure is followed when making a C scroll—just make sure that your first scroll is facing downward before you begin working on the alternate end of the stock length.

An S or C scroll can be evenly proportioned or it can have a larger section on one side. The proportions are determined by the length of stock remaining after the first forge is scrolled and by the rotation where you begin forging when starting the alternate end.

Trick of the Trade
Marking your stock ensures consistent scrolling, and a center mark will help you make uniform scrolls.

When both ends have been scrolled, but you need to close the shape up a bit in the middle, heat up the scroll and quickly quench both ends. Hammer straight down on the curl to compress the center. Quenching the ends will help keep the curves from being flattened.

Basic scrolls and twists can be fashioned into a multitude of handles.

Twisting

Twisting is a decorative technique that has many possibilities and applications. The basic rule for twisting is that the more even the heat, the more even the twist. Metals will move where they are the hottest, regardless of where you initiate a bend or twist. Any type of stock can be twisted as long as it does not have a perfectly round circumference. The metal must have at least one flat surface.

Metal stock is secured in a vise before twisting.

Stock should be inserted into the vise so that it is parallel to the floor.

There is no forging involved in twisting—only heated metal stock, a vise, and a twisting wrench. You can purchase this type of wrench from a supplier, or refer to Chapter Seven to learn how to make your own twisting wrench.

TWISTING EXPERIMENT

This first exercise is meant to show you what a piece of metal stock looks like when it is pushed to its physical limits.

Take one piece of 6 inch (15 cm) long by 3/8 inch (.075 cm) square stock and use a center punch to create 1 inch (3 cm) marks on each end of the material.

Heat the middle 4 inch (10 cm) section to a bright orange temperature. Place one end of the stock horizontally in the jaws of the vise. Use the center punch mark to determine how the tip is inserted into the jaws.

Place the jaws of the twisting wrench at the other end, with the opposing center mark lined up on the edge of the wrench facing the vise.

Stand at the vise so that you are facing the stock head-on. This way any scale that forms and falls off will not land on your forearms.

The jaws of the vise will immediately start to pull heat out of the stock. To help you work efficiently, preset the jaws of your vise to the stock width. Open the vise just enough that the material can be inserted and a half-turn of the vise handle will securely hold it in place. Remember to preset the jaws of the twisting wrench as well.

After securing the stock in the vise, place the wrench on the alternate stock end, with the wrench handle protruding horizontally. Start with either a clockwise or counter-clockwise turn, and begin to twist the metal stock. I have found that using quarter-turn increments helps keep my arms clear of the falling scale.

Keep twisting in the same direction. As the metal cools, notice what is happening. The material becomes more difficult to turn, the twists loosen up, and after a certain point, the metal will show signs of stress: surface cracks will appear on the corner edges, then the whole surface, and then, pushed past its limit, the stock will break into two pieces.

Trick of the Trade

To reduce stock distortion, it is important to keep the wrench as level as possible when twisting.

TWIST REVOLUTIONS

This exercise is meant to show you the different looks that can be created by twisting metal stock. The change in appearance is dependent upon the number of revolutions each piece has been twisted.

Use four pieces of 3/8 inch (.075 cm) -square stock, each measuring 6 inches (15 cm) long. Using soapstone, mark a 1 inch (3 cm) line from one end of each piece of stock. This line marks the location of the twisting wrench.

Very tight twisting without adequate heating causes stress cracks in the metal.

Mark a 1 inch (3 cm) line from the edge of the vise jaw. This line provides the stopping point for inserting the heated stock.

One at a time, use your tongs to grab the marked end of the stock. Heat up the middle 4 inch (10 cm) section of each stock length to a bright orange color temperature.

Use the jaws of the vise as a measuring tool.

Secure the stock in the vise up to the marked line located on the vise, and place the twisting wrench on the stock's marked line. Apply one quarter turn to the first piece of stock, then remove from the vise and quench.

The adjustable twisting wrench is secured face down at the line marked on the stock.

Follow this procedure for the three remaining pieces of stock, but increase the revolution by quarter turns. You should have four different twist revolutions when done—quarter, half, three-quarter, and a full 360 degrees.

This piece of stock has been turned halfway, or 180 degrees.

It is natural for a straight piece of metal stock to have some distortion in its alignment when subjected to twisting. You can adjust any curves by inserting the stock lengthwise into the vise jaws. Use the pressure of the jaw closing and rotate the iron after each tightening of the vise handle.

The jaws of the vise will mar or flatten the crisp edge of the twist. If you want to maintain the sharpest edges possible on your twisted stock, use a rawhide mallet and a wooden base to hammer out any distortions.

Here is a series of twists, from top to bottom: 90 degrees, 180 degrees, 270 degrees, 360 degrees, twisted until the metal cracks, and a reverse twist.

For a variation on the twist, intentionally flatten the edges by using the hammer and anvil.

Trick of the Trade

Keeping track of the marked area during heating will prevent you from wasting time trying to locate the mark when the stock is removed from the forge.

REVERSE TWIST

Use a center punch to mark an 8 inch (20 cm) piece of ³/₈ inch (.075 cm) -square stock in the center. Place the stock in the coal forge with the marked side facing upward. Heat half of the stock (up to the center mark) to a bright orange color.

Insert 1 inch (2.5 cm) of the stock into the vise jaws and place the jaws of the twisting wrench just behind the center mark (on the cool side of the stock).

Rotate the stock as much as you wish, but remember how many quarter turns you make during this first heat so that you can repeat the revolution in reverse during the second heat.

Straighten any distortions in the overall stock length, remove it from the vise, and quickly quench the twisted portion.

Reheat the metal stock, but this time place the untouched half of the stock in the fire, making sure to heat past the halfway mark and into the first section's twist.

Use a center punch to mark the center of the reversed twist.

Remove the stock from the forge and quench the existing twist. Put the stock into the vise, leaving a little of the twisted part outside of the vise grip, with the untouched half of the stock fully exposed.

Using your twisting wrench, apply the same amount of revolutions to this section, but rotate the wrench in the opposite direction of the first side's twist.

Handheld Tooling

For these next basic techniques, a hold down tool or an assistant is necessary, because you will need both hands free to work the metal. One hand will hold the tooling, with the other hand holding the hammer and striking.

Quenching the existing twist before it is placed into the vise helps prevent any marring.

Make sure that you twist the second segment in the opposite direction than the first.

CHISEL

There are two types of cuts or splits that can be made with a hand held chisel. An open split divides a piece of stock from the initial cut to the edge of the stock, making two separate tips. A closed split divides a section of stock, but leaves the entire length intact, as one piece of material. The exact same procedure is followed for both types of cuts. Different locations produce different results.

CREATING AN OPEN SPLIT

Depending upon whether you have an assistant or are using a hold-down, use an appropriate length of 1" x ¼" (2.5 x 0.5 cm) flat bar stock. Center punch 2 inches (5 cm) down from the tip of the stock and heat that area to a bright orange color.

Your chisel hand should be gloved—the radiant heat from the stock can cause burns or your hand may directly contact the stock in a hurried attempt to perform the task.

Your stock should be placed securely on the anvil face. Place your chisel over the center punch mark and prepare to strike. Your first blows should be of light to medium force—the chisel will slightly rock as you make contact.

After marking the center line of the stock with the initial chisel blows, reheat the material, return it to the anvil, and use heavier blows to cut into and past the center thickness of the stock material. You can increase the force of your hammer blows after this line has been established. Your chisel tip is less likely to move around once the notch has been made.

You will notice that the stock cools off much quicker where the line has been chiseled. This is because the material along the cut line is thinner than the rest of

As long as it is not round stock, any stock shape can be twisted. Here are some examples from left to right: round stock, round stock with opposing sides flattened, square stock, square stock with opposing corners flattened, square stock with opposing corners flattened with twist, angle iron, angle iron loosely twisted, angle iron tightly twisted, flat stock, flat stock twist.

Trick of the Trade

You can use a metal divider to score a line down the center of the flat stock before heating. This line is somewhat difficult to see, but will provide you with a guide as you divide the material with your initial hammer blows.

the stock. The thin cool line will help you guide your chisel marks when you flip the stock over to chisel the other side.

When you are ready to cut through from the other side, whether with an assistant or using a hold-down tool, place a piece of copper plate on the face of the anvil before positioning the reheated stock on the anvil face. This copper plate will help protect both the anvil surface and the chisel edge.

Line up the chisel on the cut line and begin hammering. The chisel should go through the piece completely on the backside. If it doesn't, just reheat the stock and continue chiseling until you have completely cut through.

The beginner's first cuts may be quite messy, which is why it is important to practice on sample pieces. The quicker and more efficient you perform the task, the cleaner the cut will be. All hand tools require similar trial and error practice sessions.

PUNCH AND DRIFT

Punch and drift techniques are used to make holes and openings in metal stock without removing a lot of the material. The punch is the initial hole that is made

in the stock. You can use a hand held punch or a handled punch. I prefer handled tools as I feel safer when making the heavy blows required to punch through the material.

The drift is the opening of that hole to the desired diameter and shape that is round, square, or oval.

HOLE SHAPES

Round holes are used for rivets, screws, tenons, bolts, and pretty much anything else that a round hole can be used for. Square holes are used for square stock items such as square rivets, square tenons, square nails, and pretty much anything else that a square hole can be used for.

The advantage of a square hole and insert is it more likely to remain secure than a round hole and insert, which can rotate. The disadvantage of using square shapes is that square shafts require a bit of extra work.

Oval holes are most commonly used in the eye of a hammer. The eye of a hammer is oval and the hole itself is actually tapered, with a larger opening at the bottom of the hammerhead. An oval, tapered hole provides stability to the hammer handle.

—⁓—

I never use my forging hammer when using hand held or handled tools. Do not use yours to punch, drift, or chisel stock. Save your favorite hammer for hot work only.

—⁓—

HOW TO PUNCH

Use 6 to 8 inches (15 to 20 cm) of 1" x $^1/_4$" (2.5 x 0.5 cm) -flat bar stock. Heat a 2 inch (5 cm) section at the tip of the material to the bright orange temperature color. Secure the stock to your anvil using a hold-down, and use your center punch to mark the desired location of the punch, right in the center of the portion of stock you have just heated.

Once you have made a dimple in the surface, you can use more aggressive hammer blows until the material cools off. You will not go through the metal stock in its entirety in only one heat, but do try to punch at least halfway through the material.

Reheat the stock and flip it over on your anvil. Position the stock so that the divot, the thinnest part of the stock that will cool the quickest, is located over the pritchel hole. Once it is secured in a horizontal position, use the punch and hammer through the material. A small pellet should drop out of the bottom of the pritchel hole.

When learning how to punch metal, the most common problem arises after the material has been punched on one side, turned over, and the secondary hole through the backside is not aligned with the first side. Any deviations from alignments will cause an overlap of punch edges, resulting in a sloppy hole. Do not fret though—that is why it is important to practice, practice, and practice. One day soon, you will be punching holes in one heat with a perfect pellet popping out each and every time!

The chisel, punch, drift, and other hand tools are made from high carbon steel. They have been heat-treated to ensure hardness, therefore it is very important to keep the tips of these tools cool. After each application or step, dip the tip of these tools in water. Use the tool for one heat, and then cool off the tool when the stock material is reheating. As you progress and work more efficiently, you will need to cool the tool tips more often.

I keep an empty soup can filled with water nearby when I am using these tools. It helps to remind me to keep the tools cool when I am using them.

Punching clean holes is an easy task to learn, but like most new things, you need to be patient and practice.

Distortion may occur if your pritchel hole is much bigger then the material or the punch you are working with. Make yourself a plate that has different sized holes drilled out of it. This plate can be used for a variety of hole sizes. Just place the plate over the pritchel hole before you flip your stock over and secure the plate to the anvil. There are instructions for making a pritchel plate included in Chapter Seven.

I have made pritchel plates to accommodate all of my punches.

HOW TO DRIFT

For this exercise, you will use a piece of stock that you have successfully punched through, a drift tool, and a drift plate.

When you select a drift, notice that the tool has a long taper on one end and a short taper on the other end. The long taper of the drift is the end that will be driven through the punched hole.

As you reheat the punched area of your stock material to a bright orange color temperature, set up your pritchel plate so that the hole which measures the same width as the thickest part of the drift is located directly over the pritchel hole.

Important Things to Remember when Drifting

1. Always work when the metal is heated to a bright orange color temperature.

2. Never pick up the drift by the tip after it has been driven through the stock.

3. If the drift gets stuck, flip over the stock and tap out the tool.

4. Cool the tip of the tool after each use.

TOOL USAGE AND FORGING TECHNIQUES

89

PARTIAL DRIFT FOR MAKING SMALL HOLES

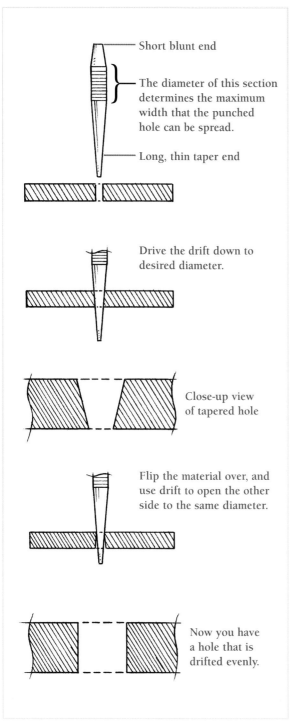

Short blunt end

The diameter of this section determines the maximum width that the punched hole can be spread.

Long, thin taper end

Drive the drift down to desired diameter.

Close-up view of tapered hole

Flip the material over, and use drift to open the other side to the same diameter.

Now you have a hole that is drifted evenly.

A cross section view of the drifting process.

Secure the stock on the anvil so that the holes of the stock and the drift plate line up. Insert the long taper end of your drift into the hole and hammer down on the drift. The thickest part of the drift is the maximum opening that will be spread through the punched hole.

Your objective is to hammer the drift completely through the hole. When done successfully, the drift should fall through the pritchel hole once the widest part of the drift has cleared the punched hole.

If the drift happens to get stuck during the process, pick up the stock and turn it over. With the stock laying flat on the anvil and the stuck drift located just of the edge of the anvil, hammer on the long taper until the drift is released.

If necessary, reheat the stock in the forge, align the drift, punched hole, and pritchel hole, and continue with your hammering. The processes of moving metal will be better understood with experience. Metal moves like clay, a material many of us are familiar with. It is not unheard of for experienced smiths to use clay as a reference for experimentation and observation, before deciding how to approach a project at their lighted forge. Remember: The more you know, the more you *know*.

The hole to be drifted is lined up over the pritchel hole.

A drift can be dislodged from your metal material by turning the stock upside down and hammering down on the taper.

Make a depression with a grinder or carve it out of the wood. The shape should be larger than the disk you are sinking. When first learning how to sink, start off with smaller discs. A 3 inch (8 cm) disc makes an excellent candle cup that can be incorporated into other projects. Larger blanks can be used to create bowls.

In addition to suppliers, discs are available as a by-product from companies that specialize in cutting or punch-pressing steel. When I started out, I used a cutting torch to make circles for sinking. Today, I use a plasma cutter and template to make any size disc that I need.

1. The key to a good sink is to have a hot, evenly heated disc, also called a blank. Once the material starts to cool, hammering will leave little dimples—only hammer when the heated material is yellow-orange in appearance.

2. Scalloping the edges using a ball peen is an easy and decorative way to treat the edges of a dish before sinking.

3. If you do not have a swage block, you can use a concave surface created on a log stump. To decrease smoke and prevent any fire flare-ups, soak the surface of the wood for a few hours before using it.

CHAPTER SIX

FORGE WELDING AND OTHER ASSEMBLAGE TECHNIQUES

This chapter concentrates on how several pieces of forged iron are put together to perform a particular function. Some methods are simple, while others are tricky. Many blacksmiths opt to use modern equipment, such as electric welders. However, it is beneficial in all aspects of your metalworking to know as much as you can about traditional joinery skills.

Forge Welding

Forge welding, also referred to as fire welding, is the process of uniting two or more pieces of metal through the application of heat and hammer. When the proper welding temperature has been achieved, two pieces of steel stock can be fused together with hammer blows. Forge welding is not a difficult process. It can be characterized by a combination of intimidation and excitement. Your chance of being burned by the materials during forge welding is somewhat high—though burning yourself is not a requirement or a prerequisite to a good weld. By maintaining your focus and staying calm, you will learn how it feels to connect with the iron, not simply manipulate it.

Forge welding with a coal forge offers smiths two advantages over gas forges and electric welding:

1. Forge welding fuses the entire contact surface, while modern gas and arc welding only fuse the adjoining surfaces of two pieces of metal.

2. Some gas forges are not capable of reaching welding temperatures that a properly maintained coal forge fire can provide. Gas and propane forges have a tendency to produce more fire scale on metal than coal fires.

Therefore, all of the exercises in this book have been completed using a coal forge.

Forge Welding Fire Instructions

Before setting up a forge welding fire, make sure that your coal forge has been cleared of any clinkers and ash. The most common fire used to forge weld is a chamber-shaped or beehive fire. This formation will allow you to observe the metal stock as it heats, and an enclosed "oven" concentrates the heat on the stock in the chamber.

A beehive fire is very similar in formation to a banked fire. When a fire is banked, the building up of wet coal on top of burning coal insulates and keeps

the embers slowly burning for a long period of time. There is not a continual forced air source, just additional insulation.

Beehive fires have the same layered technique, but the airflow is constant, which creates a very hot center for forge welding. The outer wet layer creates a shell. This barrier is poked open to create an entrance for your stock. The entrance is located on the front and near the bottom of the mound, where the fire is white hot.

Follow the same start up procedure that you used when building a regular forging fire. As you rake coal into the fire, pat down the mound with the bottom of the shovel. The goal is to create a very hot and compacted heat source. Once a fire has been established, increase the blower and start adding moistened coal to the fire. As the wet coal burns, it will solidify and surround your fire with a hard igloo-shaped chamber. Continue adding wet coal and pat it down with the shovel. The overall height of the mound of coke should be equal to the depth of the fire box.

The center of this beehive is perfect for forge welding.

The interior of your compacted coal pile has transformed into coke. This fuel will provide a clean, hot fire, which is essential for forge welding. While maintaining the overall shape of your igloo, poke a horizontal access and viewing vent into the front of the mound.

Upon adding coke fuel, increase the blower until the fire inside the chamber takes on a white hot appearance. Remember to shut down the blower before proceeding with the actual forge welding—the increase in air circulation increases the rate of oxidation.

Scarfing

Before two pieces of metal can be forge welded, you must prepare the mating or contact surfaces so that they can be successfully melded together. Scarfing is the process of upsetting the tips of two pieces of stock with angled, slightly bulged surfaces. The purpose of hammering the end or edge of a piece of metal stock is to create a diagonal, bulged surface. Scarfing also builds up the mass of material that will be lost in the heating and hammering process.

The diagonal surface increases the contact surface area of the weld. The convex surface helps to ensure that the center of the joint is fused before the edges, and it allows for any impurities, such as slag, oxides, and welding flux, to be expelled during the welding process. This allows for a stronger connection between the two pieces of material.

Your stock ends should be upsetted before they are scarfed. This increase in mass will help you maintain the original thickness of your steel after the actual welding process is achieved.

Long, thin scarfs should be avoided. An overly drawn out scarf is susceptible to burning up and has difficulty maintaining the proper heat temperature because it loses its heat rapidly. A finished scarf end should measure out to approximately $1\frac{1}{2}$ times the thickness of the original stock material.

Trick of the Trade
You need to remove any debris that has collected inside the bottom of the pot before attempting to forge weld. It is imperative that your welding fire be as clean and as hot as possible. The fuel used for welding should be coke. After removing the clinkers from the chamber, you can begin chipping the outer shell of coke inside the chamber.

SCARFING: UPSETTING, ANGLING, REFINING, CONNECTING

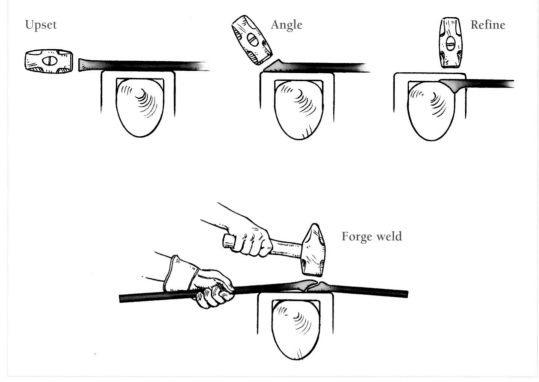

Upset   Angle   Refine

Forge weld

The scarfing process involves upsetting, angling, and refining before a forge weld can be made.

A standard igloo-shaped forging fire is used for the exercise. Use a 20 inch (51 cm) length of ³/₈-inch (1 cm) -square stock (round stock can be scarfed but it has a tendency to roll, making it more difficult to learn this technique). Start by heating the tip (¹/₂ inch [1 cm] or less) of one piece of stock to a bright orange color. Remember, if the heat is longer than ¹/₂ inch (1 cm), quickly pour a stream of water on the back-side of the material to cool it off.

Place the heated tip over the far side of the anvil face and bring your hammer straight down on the tip of the stock. These are called back-up blows. Rotate the stock 180 degrees while hammering every few blows until you see the end compress and become larger than the stock size.

Hold your stock material nearly flat on the face of the anvil and use your hammer to move the bulge to one side of the tip.

Reheat the end (approximately 1¹/₂ inches [3.5 cm] of one piece of stock to the bright orange color. Place the heated end flat on the far side of the anvil face. Use back blows, positioning your hammer face so that it is making contact at a 45 degree angle with the upsetted material surface. Position the scarf with the large bulge against the round edge of the anvil and forge its convex.

All shaped metal stocks can be scarfed but only round stock scarfs come to a point. Rectangular and square stock scarfs have a straight edge with a slight radius.

Forge Welding Temperature and Appearance

The optimum temperature for forge welding mild steel is 2300°F (1260°C). At welding heat, this material has a molten surface and a very soft internal structure. A common mistake of beginning smiths is to overuse the blower of the forge in an effort to increase their fire intensity. Air flow increases the rate of oxidation. A fire scale surface can not be forge welded.

It is important not to overheat the metal and to work efficiently once a welding heat has been achieved. Try to avoid repeated weld heats of steel that you intend to fire forge as reheating increases the difficulty of getting the materials to adhere to each other.

BURN BABY BURN

So let's just experience the whole heat and temperature process by intentionally burning a piece of stock measuring about 5" (13 cm) long x $^1/_2$" (1 cm) diameter, square, or round. Build your fire and place one half of the stock into the fire. Be sure to wear your didymium safety glasses. Watch what happens, but do not stare intently. You will notice that as the color of the metal stock becomes lighter, the surface gains a glasslike appearance. Watch for the initial sparks, and in short time, the sparks will become intense as the metal begins to melt.

Successful forge welding is a quick process. By watching this melting process on practice pieces, you will have a better understanding of the limited time frame in which heated metal can be forge welded together.

Place the material (i.e. scarfed surface) to be forge welded into the fire. Position the stock horizontally, and carefully rotate the material to make sure that the heat is being evenly applied. Once the material has a bright orange color heat, carefully rotate the stock so the mating surfaces are facing upward and sprinkle flux onto the scarfed surfaces.

As the metal continues to heat do not increase the blower in an attempt to accelerate the fire temperature—more air causes more oxidation. Once a welding temperature (sparking yellow or white appearance) has been achieved, quickly remove the metal from the fire. Lift the material vertically and out from the fire— do not drag it through your coals. Once removed from the forge, use your wire brush to remove any impurities on the contact surfaces and strike the stock on the edge of the anvil to pop off any excess flux.

Your stock is now ready to be forge welded.

Different Types of Forge Welds

FAGOT WELD

A fagot weld is probably the easiest forge weld to perform. It is created without having to upset your material and a scarfed edge is not mandatory. The word fagot dates to the 14th century and refers to the bundling of sticks. Fagot welds consist of either a bundle of iron stock or one piece of bar stock bent back on itself. Fagot welds can be used to recycle scrap materials into a thicker piece of stock or they can be used to increase the mass at the end of a piece of stock without upsetting.

For this exercise, obtain a 20" (51 cm) length of $^3/_8$" (1 cm) -square stock. Using the beehive fire, heat approximately 5 inches (13 cm) of the tip to a bright orange welding temperature.

WHAT THE FLUX IS FLUX?

Flux is a powdered compound consisting of either borax or a combination of borax and other materials. It is applied to the mating surfaces of mild and carbon steels during the forge welding process. Flux liquefies and removes any scaling that has occurred during the heating process and protects the metal from any further oxidation.

Oxidation is a normal occurrence during the forge heating process, but steel cannot be forge welded when scale is present. Scaled steel has a higher melting point than unscaled steel, but through a chemical process, flux lowers the melting temperature of scale, thus allowing steel to be welded at a somewhat lower temperature. Once applied, flux melts and flows into the tightest cracks, removing any oxide that has already formed, and coats the exposed surfaces to stop any further scaling.

Flux can be applied to the welding surface while the stock remains in the fire or you can remove the material from the fire and sprinkle it on. I leave the

stock in the fire—it's the easiest and fastest way. One of the first projects presented in the back of this book shows you how to make a spoon. Make a long handled flux spoon and you will be set.

As the flux begins to melt you will notice that the surface looks wet and fluid; this is called a slippery welding temperature. Soon after, the surface will take on a bright yellow or white appearance and sparks will begin. This means that your material has reached a semimolten state, that the surface has begun to burn slightly, and that it is time to forge the weld.

Place 3 inches (8 cm) of this heated portion over a hot cut hardy tool and hammer down until the stock is cut one-half of the way through.

Position the stock, with the cut mark facing upwards, on the far edge of the anvil face, and hammer the protruding portion downwards.

Bring the entire heated section of the stock to the anvil surface and continue hammering until the stock bends back upon itself and the two sides meet.

Return the stock to the fire and bring it up to a yellow-orange forging temperature. Sprinkle some flux on both sides of the seam and return the stock to the fire.

As it is heating up to the slippery welding temperature, prepare for the upcoming steps. Make sure that your wire brush is waiting on the anvil, as well as your hammer.

When the sparks start to pop out of the fire and a proper welding temperature color has appeared (sparking yellow and white), carefully and quickly remove the stock from the forge and use the wire brush to remove any fire scale and excess flux that may be on the material.

Return the stock to the anvil face. The first blows are on the top and bottom, leaving the seamed sides open to push out any impurities. The first few hits of the hammer should occur quickly, dead on, with medium to light blows. This allows the moltening material to begin to stick. Heavy blows will blow the molten material out of the sides of the scarf, losing the initial weld. Heavy blows should occur only after the initial connection has been made.

Because fagot welds are easy to perform, they are the perfect exercise to practice while learning how to identify a proper welding temperature color.

LOOP OR EYE WELD

A loop weld is a fairly simple procedure that requires only one piece of stock and one scarfed end. This weld can be performed on all types of stock materials, but I am going to explain how to do it with round stock. The loop weld technique is incorporated into numerous forging projects. Its shape makes a nice grip for your hand and also provides a hanger. Forge fire tools and fireplace tools are common examples of utilitarian metalwork that incorporates a loop weld.

For this exercise, cut a 30 inch (76 cm) length of 3/8 inch (.075 cm) -round stock. Heat the end of the metal (about 1 inch [3 cm]) to a bright orange forging temperature and taper.

Return the stock to your fire and heat the tapered end of the stock (approximately 10 inches [25 cm]) to the forging color temperature. Bend this portion over the horn until the tapered tip meets up with the stock. Pinch the two pieces together but try to maintain a space between them.

Return the stock to your fire and heat the area between the bulge and the scarfed tip. Use your anvil horn to shape this section into a loop. Keep hammering until the tip meets the section of upset/bulged stock.

The loop shape makes it a little difficult to return the metal stock to the fire. Gently nudge the coals of your beehive fire with a rake and place the looped end of your stock into the coals, with the area to be welded right in the center of the fire. It is best to apply the flux before putting the stock in the fire. Bring up the stock color temperature to a sparking yellow/white.

After removing the stock from the forge fire, use a wire brush to quickly remove any scale, then bring the loop to the anvil face. Your first hammer blow should occur at the thickest area of the connection—right at the heel of your taper. Remember to use controlled hammer strikes. Hammer the sides of the weld by rotating the material.

After the forge weld has been completed, return the loop to the fire, reheat, and use the horn of your anvil to open up and shape the loop.

LAP WELD

Lap welding is the process of joining two scarfed edges together. Because this weld requires two scarfed edges, it is important that both scarfs are forged to the same length and angled surface. Otherwise, you will not have a smooth transition between stock. Since two separate pieces are being joined, this type of weld requires a bit more choreography.

For this exercise, use two pieces of 3/8-inch (.075 cm) square stock. Cut one at 5 inches (13 cm) and the other at 20 inches (51 cm). The longer piece of stock can be held with your hand and the shorter piece will require tongs.

Heat the end of each piece of metal (about 1 inch [2.5 cm]) to a bright orange forging temperature and upset. Reheat to forging color and scarf the upsetted end of each piece of your metal stock.

Return the pieces of stock to the fire, following the flux application process, and heat the metal to the sparking yellow/white forge welding temperature.

Your dominant hand will hold the short piece secured in the tongs and your passive hand will grip the longer length of material. Remove both pieces from the fire.

Place the short piece on the face of the anvil, scarf side up. With the short piece in position, place the long piece, scarf side down, over the first. When the two scarfed surfaces make contact, they will stick together. Once you see that the tips are aligned, with both mating surfaces touching, drop the tongs and pick up the hammer.

Strike down a few times before rotating the stock, then use rapid, heavy blows while rotating the stock. Continue until the two pieces appear to be connected throughout the length of the scarfs. Remember that you need to maintain a uniform thickness. Do not hammer once the welding temperature color has diminished. Once the color is gone, you will be moving the metal, not welding the metal together.

You have just forge welded two separate pieces of steel stock. To test the strength of your weld, place the materials in the grip of your vise just below the weld. Use your hammer and strike a couple of heavy blows. A strong weld will bend without breaking apart.

T WELD AND L WELD

The T weld and L weld follow the same process as a lap weld except the joined metal is connected in different configurations: T welds are used to perpendicularly join two pieces of metal stock. L welds connect two stock ends to create a 90 degree angle.

There are other techniques that can be used to join two or more pieces of metal rather than forge welding. These connections are different than forge welding because the materials are not melded together at high temperatures.

Rivets

Riveting is the process of creating a stationary or pivoted joint between two or more metal surfaces. Two pieces of metal that are going to be riveted together have holes punched or drilled out of them. The rivet diameter is slightly smaller than the hole in the stock. One end of the rivet has a head to catch hold of both pieces of material. The other end, which is the shank, is heated and hammered down or just hammered cold. If the rivet is set cold, the shank of the rivet is flattened. If the rivet is set hot, a shaped rivet head can be forged from the shank to match the rivet head.

Rivets are available ready-made in a variety of head shapes, as well as a wide range of diameters and lengths—or you can make your own.

Trick of the Trade
The heads of mass-produced rivets can be dressed or decorated to minimize their manufactured look.

FINISHING A RIVET END

A. Rivet head

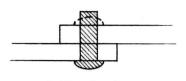

B. Countersink

This illustration shows two ways that a rivet can be set. (A) shows a traditional rivet head while (B) shows the incorporation of a counter sunk hole. The mass of the rivet is hammered into the bevel area, with the remainder filed off, leaving a flush surface. If both sides of the rivet are countersunk, it is called an invisible rivet.

For a flush rivet head, one piece of material needs to be countersunk. The excess rivet that would normally protrude out from the surface will be hammered inside the divot of the countersink.

One round shank rivet through metal stock will create a pivot, while two or more round shank rivets through the same pieces of metal stock will make the connection stationary.

To prevent movement of a single rivet connection, insert a square rivet through square holes.

Mortise and Tenon

A tenon is a bolt-like end forged on one piece of stock that is inserted through the hole (mortise) of a different piece of metal, and then it is headed, like a rivet. Handmade rivets are basically tenons with short heads.

Tenons require a clean, sharp shoulder to rest properly on the other piece of metal's surface. A soft-shouldered tenon will rock once it is headed into another piece of metal.

In order to finish a tenon, a monkey tool is used. Monkey tools are in available in a vast array of shapes and sizes. A monkey tool slips over a heated tenon and it is driven into it with quick rotating blows to drive the end into the stock. Tools for round tenons can be easily made by drilling a blind hole centrally into the end of a short piece of tool steel stock.

Another way to dress the shoulder of the tenon is to drive the tenoned pieced down into a plate that has the same size diameter hole as the tenon diameter.

Place the proper size drill hole over the pritchel and put the heated tenon through both. Hammer down on the tenon piece to compact the shoulder.

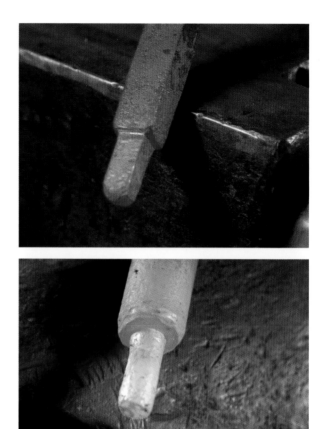

Tenons can be made either square (top) or round.

Shrinking

Shrinking is the process of joining two pieces of metal by inserting a cold piece into a hole in a hot piece of iron. The hot iron shrinks as it is cooled and holds the cold piece almost as tightly as a weld.

Heating causes one piece of metal to contract or expand onto the other, producing pressure that then holds the two pieces together.

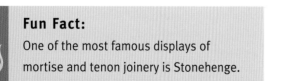

Fun Fact:
One of the most famous displays of mortise and tenon joinery is Stonehenge.

Monkey tools are used to dress tenons.

Collars

Ornamental ironwork, especially scrollwork, is commonly assembled with the use of collars. Collars are also called clips or bands. A collar is simply a hot piece of metal wrapped around two or more pieces of ironwork to hold them together. The most common collars are made from rectangular stock.

Collars are sized and partially formed before assembly with the use of a mandrel or the edge of the anvil. There are two basic types of collars:

Scarf collar—The edges of each end of the collar are flattened so that when they meet after wrapping around the stock, an even, angled edge is formed.

Overlap collar—Just like the name implies, the wrapped edge lies on top of the first edge. This type of collar is easier to create but does not appear as refined as a scarfed collar.

Although some math skill is required for collaring, here is the easiest way to estimate it. Your first collars may need some modification, but you can start off using the formula that follows.

(Thickness of material to be joined x 4)

+ (Height of material to be joined x 2)

+ (Thickness of collar material x 2)

Example: Let's say that you have two scrolls that you want to join with a collar that is $1/8$-inch (0.3 cm) thick. The scrolls are made from $1/2$-inch (1 cm) square stock.

$(1/2 \times 4) + (1/2 \times 2) + (1/8 \times 2) =$

$4/2 + 1 + 2/8 =$

$2 + 1 + 1/4 = 3 \, 1/4$

Your collar length should be $3^{1}/4$ inches (8.3 cm)

> **Trick of the Trade**
> This process can be performed on both square and round stock, but it is much more difficult to make a permanent, stationary collar on round stock materials. Flatten an edge around the area of the round stock where the collar will be applied.

Another way I found to measure the length of a collar is to use a cloth tape measure.

I always make one collar first and check the fitting before continuing with the production of the remaining collars. I wrap it around the two pieces I want to join and add the thickness of the collar material times two.

To form the collar, heat the material and wrap it around the mandrel. The closing ends need to be determined first—where will the seam be located? If you are making a trivet, the seams should be facing downward. If the scrolls are for a window grille that can be viewed from both sides, the seams should be located on the edge of a scroll. I use an oxy-acetylene torch to execute the final isolate heat, and then hammer the collar into place.

Securing collars to scrolls can be somewhat difficult to do by yourself. Traditional work usually implies that there are extra hands of apprentices and secondary smiths available to assist.

For this collar exercise, use a piece of ⅜-inch (.075 cm) copper tubing. First collapse the tubing by flattening the whole length or by using the cross peen of a small hammer to collapse the center. This should not be done hot since copper is a soft material. Once you have pinched the center, it will need to be annealed or heated to resoften the material.

As a solo smith, I have had better success with collars when they are applied decoratively rather than as the primary means of assemblage. I have also used softer material than mild steel to create collars. I like using copper because of its ease in forming around scrollwork and the color contrast between the two metals.

The second 90 degree bend can be formed on the mandrel or in the jaws of a small vise.

As you have now experienced, I wasn't kidding about some of these assembly techniques being tricky. It really helps to have another person who is equally interested to offer assistance and support. Many things can be made traditionally by solo smiths but you have to remember that most blacksmith shops "in the good old days" had more people working in the smithy then just the master smith. Sharing the learning process has many personal and professional benefits, including life-long friendships and thwarted romances.

Wraps

The wrap material is smaller than the forged items to be held together. When the hot metal cools and contracts, it grips the cold stock securely. It is difficult to make a secure wrap without the use of modern welding equipment (I call this Zap and Wrap), but this technique makes lovely decorative, rather than structural, joinery.

Wrapping with Rods

Heating one piece of metal and wrapping it around a group of unheated pieces of metal creates a wrap.

1. Collapse the copper tubing with the cross peen of a small hammer.

2. To form the collar, bend the collapsed tubing over the edge of the anvil or use a mandrel. This will make the first 90 degree bend.

3. The second 90 degree bend can be formed on the mandrel or in the jaws of a small vise.

4. Because copper is a soft metal, you can start the last 90 degree bend using your hands.

5. Finish the bending with the cross peen of a small hammer.

6. You can also use vise grips to squeeze the collar together before hammering it closed.

CHAPTER SEVEN

MAKING YOUR OWN TOOLING

You can make many of your own tools, or you can purchase them from manufacturers or independent blacksmiths who make and sell the tools. The question you need to ask yourself is, "where do you want to start with your own blacksmithing?" Some folks want to first learn the actual movement of hot metal. They want to concentrate on the forging processes before attempting to make their own tools. Some folks feel that a better understanding of the forging processes comes along with the making of their own tools.

Classes and tooling are not cheap, and if you have more time than money, you may want to incorporate tool making into your initial forging project experiences.

—⁂—

Personally, I wanted to start making things before tooling. It brought me more satisfaction to create a piece for my home or as a gift, than to make tooling. I also had the opportunity to do my beginning work in a well-equipped blacksmith shop.

—⁂—

This book provides you with many resources for classes, tool suppliers, or instruction on making your own tools. You can decide what combination works best for your needs and interest.

Resources Needed to Make Your Own Tools

Some of the tooling in this chapter can be made without the use of any modern technology, while others require the assistance of a striker, and some require the use of modern equipment.

The electric welder has become an integral part of most blacksmithing shops today. If you do not have the resources to hire a welder or you do not know someone who welds, then purchasing your own is an option.

Today, you can find just about any tool you need available for purchase. There are skilled blacksmiths who forge tooling as part of their business. There's something special about making your own art with your own handmade tools.

Although welding is not a necessity to make a bending fork, you will need access to a set of cutting torches and tanks in order to cut the pattern out of steel plate. A drill press is needed to make a pritchel plate.

The first selection of tools can be made working alone with a hammer, anvil, and forge.

Drift

The drift is the easiest tool to make because it can be forged out of mild or hard steel. Its shape is so basic that someone might mistake it for an unfinished taper project. Although drifts can be forged to create openings of various sizes, the basic shape is always the same: One side has a long taper with a small point on the end and the other side is a short taper with a very blunt end. The width of the stock material used determines the maximum diameter of the drift you are going to forge. For a ½ inch (1 cm) -round drift, use ½ inch (1 cm) -round stock.

Because your drift will only be used on orange hot steel, it is not imperative that the drift be made from tool steel. The drift tip may need to be dressed now and again, but this task requires very little effort. Mild steel stock will work fine for this tool.

Start with a 6 inch (15 cm) length of ½ inch (1 cm) -round stock and taper one-half of its length to a gradual thin taper, no larger then ⅛ inch (0.3 cm) diameter at the tip.

Heat the other end and forge a short taper on that tip. There should be a middle section of your stock material that has not been forged. This is the part that becomes the drift—it determines the maximum diameter that a punched hole can be spread.

Next, make yourself a square drift. Follow the same procedure used for the first exercise.

Trick of the Trade

You can use a drift that is larger than the desired hole size, just don't drive the drift all of the way through. Stop when the taper opens up the hole to the diameter you want, then turn the stock material upside down and tap the drift out. You may need to reheat the stock and run the drift through the backside of the punched hole. This will provide you with a drift opening that is uniform on both sides.

A simple twisted handle can be added to a hand held punch if you desire.

Handheld Punch

A punch can either be handheld or attached to a handle. The handle can be made of wood like a hammer, or a piece of iron can be wrapped around the punch—this is called rodded. Punches should be made from high carbon steel. Remember that the appropriate forging color temperature for high carbon steel is a bright orange-yellow. It should be heated a bit longer than mild steel.

For this exercise, you can use a 6 inch (15 cm) length of ½ inch (1 cm) -round or square high carbon steel and heat it in the forge.

Trick of the Trade

Once you become familiar with the different grades of carbon steel, you will notice that there are many materials commonly made of high carbon steel that can be recycled into tools. A good example is coil springs. Earlier in chapter three, I wrote about how to spark test metal. High carbon steel emits light patterns that are bright, quick, and light, with very short tails. You can use a coil spring to make a punch. Run a spark test to verify that it is high carbon steel before proceeding. Instead of trying to straighten the entire coil, use a cloth tape measure to determine how much is needed, and use a hot cut torch or a chop saw. Heat the coil to a bright orange-yellow color temperature and straighten it out.

Forge the stock so that it has a four-sided, but not sharp-cornered, square diameter. The next step is to flatten the corners so that you have a slight octagonal shape. This provides extra-strength to the hand tool.

Taper one end down to an oval shape. The taper does not need to be very long, but the tip should be no wider than 3/16 inch (4.5 mm) or so. The other end should be blunted and slightly domed to provide a maximum amount of hitting surface.

Because the tool is made from high carbon steel it will need to be heat treated. Please refer to the end of this chapter for information on the proper heat treating and hardening of high carbon steel.

Handheld Slit Chisel

The handheld slit chisel is used to make straight line cuts. It has a slightly rounded edge that allows it to be rocked along the stock material, running marks down the stock. A slit chisel can also be used to open up stock for drifting, but unlike the punch, a slit chisel doesn't remove any of the stock material.

A handheld chisel is short, about 7 inches (18 cm) long, with a slight domed end for hitting and an octagonal shaft. The cutting edge is flat, similar to the beginning of a fish tail scroll. It has a long thin taper that is rounded ever so slightly.

All chisels are made in pretty much the same manner: they all have a wide end for striking and an octagonal shaft.

You should make this tool out of high carbon steel. It will need to be heat treated. Go ahead and forge all of your handheld tools and then heat treat them all at the same time.

Trick of the Trade

Instead of making an entirely new chisel, modify an old one to suit your needs.

Twisting Bar

Each twisting bar can bend up to two different square stock sizes between its S-shaped jaws. Start an 18-inch (46 cm) piece of 1/2 inch (1 cm) -square stock. Mark the center of the material with a punch.

Heat up one side of the marked metal stock, close to the centerline, and bend the material upon itself so that a piece of 1/4 inch (0.5 cm) -square stock fits in the gap.

Heat the second central portion of the material and bend it back in the opposite direction so that a piece of 3/8 inch (1 cm) -square stock can be inserted into the gap.

For twisting bars that hold larger square stock, use larger stock material. For example, to bend 1/2 inch (1 cm) -square stock and 5/8 inch (1.5 cm) –square stock, use 1 inch (3 cm) thick material stock. Just make sure that the stock material you are using is wider than the stock sizes you intend to bend.

TWISTING BAR

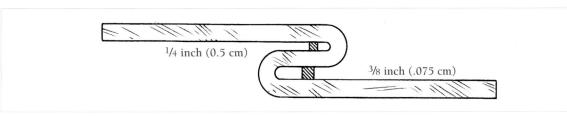

1/4 inch (0.5 cm)

3/8 inch (.075 cm)

1. Forge a button end by upsetting the tip, then flattening it to create a larger surface area to hold down your work.

2. Draw out a bridge about 3 inches (8 cm) long.

Hold Fast, Hold Down

The hold fast, hold down tool is used to secure stock to the anvil's face. The tool is inserted in the pritchel hole, placed over the metal stock, and tapped down, creating tension.

The tension of it being stuck in the hole, with its outer arm pressing down against the anvil face, provides the perfect tool for the solitary smith working on smaller projects that would otherwise require an extra hand. Whatever is placed between the anvil and the hold down tool is secured until you tap the clip sideways and break the tension.

A square shank jams much better into the pritchel round pritchel hole, but either a square or round shank will work.

Start with a 12 inch (30 cm) piece of 5/8-inch (1.5 cm) -round or square stock. The bridge can be tapered even or left with more material on the sides.

To Use: Place a piece of hot metal on the face of the anvil. Insert the hold fast tool into the pritchel hole, making contact between its button tip and your stock material. Tap down at the point where the bridge and shank meet in order to create tension.

The biggest obstacle in making your hardy tools is the material stock sizes you have to work with—you

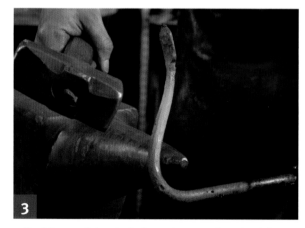

3. Bend the remaining stock at a 90 degree angle and curl the bridge so that the button end is perpendicular to the shaft.

4. Hot materials can be easily secured to your anvil face with a hold down tool.

will be working with more massive materials than those typically used in forging exercises. Anvil tools are easier to make if you have a striker to help you. The extra muscle and sledge comes in handy due to the additional force needed to forge larger stock tool steel.

HARDY TOOLS

The size of the hardy hole in your anvil will determine the appropriate shank size of all of your hardy tools. Larger anvils have a 1 inch (3 cm) -square or slightly larger hardy hole. This works well since 1-inch (3 cm) -thick square stock is widely available.

It is important to make sure that your hardy shanks fit into the hole without being too loose. Shanks that are too tight can be easily corrected by grinding or forging.

FORGING A HARDY TOOL SHAFT

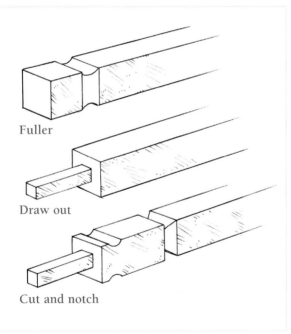

Fuller

Draw out

Cut and notch

Hot Cut Hardy

Start with square stock that is slightly bigger than the size of the hardy hole. If the stock material is substantially larger then the hole, you will have more work in drawing out the shank.

Using a spring fuller, a large guillotine, or a striker with a top and bottom fuller set, fuller all four sides evenly, making sure that the depth of the fuller is not smaller then the hardy hole opening.

Draw out the tip to form the shank, making sure that it is a tight fit and not easily dropped into the hardy hole. The shank should be at least 2 inches (5 cm) long, and it does not need to be tapered.

The second fuller marks are only on two opposing sides. These marks establish the shoulder. Place the fuller marks about 1/2 inch (1 cm) from the drop that starts the shank.

The next step is to cut off the piece from the parent stock. Cut about 1 1/2 inches (4 cm) down from the shoulder marks. This will provide you with enough material to draw out for the cutting edge of the actual hot cut tool.

Reheat the shank and shoulder area for its final fitting into the hardy hole. Be prepared with a short 8 inch (20 cm) piece of pipe or round stock to dislodge the shank from underneath, should it get jammed in the hardy hole.

This fitting step can be done in one of two ways: Your hardy tool can be finished so that it fits only one way into the hardy hole, or it can be made to fit into the hole universally. The benefit of having one stationary position is that it will provide a very secure fit. Since the hardy hole itself is not perfectly square, the single position fitting is created by hammering down on the newly cut end while the shank is at a yellow color temperature. Hammer it until the shank is in the hole up to its shoulder.

The drawbacks of having one stationary position in

MAKING A HOT CUT HARDY

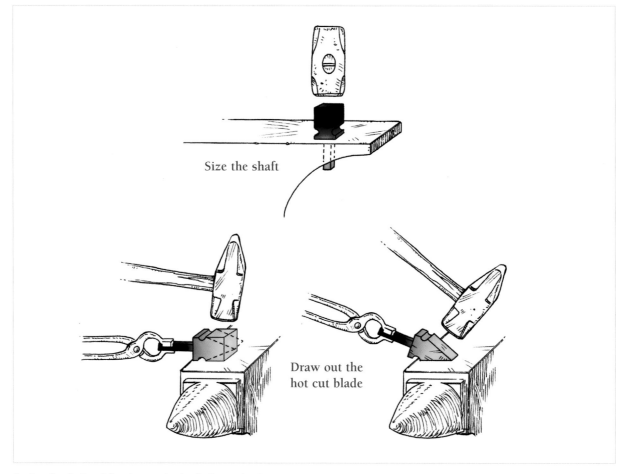

Size the shaft

Draw out the hot cut blade

Setting the shaft and drawing out the tip of a hot cut hardy.

which it can be inserted is that if you accidentally insert it improperly, the tool may become jammed.

The hot cut's edge should be parallel to the long edge of the anvil's face. It is very important that your initial setting of the tool has the two sided fuller marks running in the same direction as what the drawn-out edge will be.

To create an "all position" hardy hot cut, simply follow the same steps as in the single position, but rotate 90 degrees and hammer the shaft into the hole again. Keep lifting, rotating, and hammering until the hardy slips into the hole from all directions.

The benefit of an all position hardy is that it has no chance of being jammed or inserted wrong. The

drawback is that the fit is not as secure as the single, stationary position—there is still a little bit of movement with an all-position hardy tool.

Once you have decided and established the shank's positioning, heat the mass on the opposite end to a yellow-orange color temperature, and draw it out to a wedge taper. Remember that the hot cut wedge taper is slightly longer than the cold cut wedge taper. Your hot cut should have a narrow ridge before forging the final edge.

Once you have finished this tool, do not forget that it needs to be properly heat treated. Directions for heat treating are at the end of this chapter.

Cold Cut Hardy

Follow the same process that you used to make the hot cut hardy, except when it comes to drawing out the cold cut wedge, it should be shaped more stout and compact than the hot cut. A cold cut wedge has less tapering.

Reminder: As I wrote earlier, the cold cut is a tool that is used to separate a smaller piece from its parent stock while the material is cold. Its function is to nick the edges of the material enough that you can manually snap the material into two pieces. As a beginner, you may choose to cut stock with another, more modern method—a chop saw, an electric band saw, a cut-off wheel on your grinder, air tools—there are many options available for you.

These hardy tool project instructions require the use of modern equipment such as an electric welder, drill press, and a torch cutter. The shank of these hardy tools can be made to fit universally, in any position, since they are not cutting tools.

Nail Header

The nail header is a tool that rounds the head of a square tapered nail. The header is domed to allow the hammer face to make slightly angled contact with the nails—creating a four-faceted or rose head nail.

Because the nail header takes a lot of impact, it should be made from tool steel. A leaf spring works great for this project, but remember that all harder steel alloys are more difficult to forge and drift. When using tool steel, all forging should be performed when the metal is heated to a yellow-orange color temperature.

Using the cross peen of your hammer, draw down the center portion, top side only, in between the two ends. Keep the bottom surface flat.

Heat one rounded end and hammer the edges downward to create a high point in the center of the mound.

Reheat and punch a square hole through the center. This hole should be no larger than 1/8 inch (0.3 cm) square. Heat the material again and from the bottom,

MAKING A NAIL

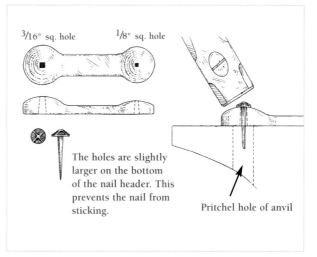

3/16" sq. hole   1/8" sq. hole

The holes are slightly larger on the bottom of the nail header. This prevents the nail from sticking.

Pritchel hole of anvil

run a square drift up thorough the hole. Do not quench—allow the material to cool naturally.

Heat the other end to form a mound in the same fashion. After punching a square hole through, drift the hole to be slightly larger than the first hole, no bigger than 3/16 inch to 1/2 inch (4.8 mm to 1.3 cm) -square.

Reheat and drift the underneath side to make the tapered hole—just make sure that the larger opening is on the bottom.

When the piece has cooled down, use a flap disc and grinder to shape, smooth, and round the mound.

Making nails is a good way to learn basic techniques. Each nail requires tapering, hot cutting, upsetting, and decorative-angled hammer blows.

To begin, draw out a 1/2 inch (1.3 cm) section of 1/8 inch (.03 cm) -square stock. Hot cut almost completely through the parent stock, leaving enough material to make the head of the nail.

Reheat and place the point into the nail header, and twist off from the parent stock. Place the nail and header over the pritchel hole and compress the exposed stock straight down. The last four blows should be angled, so the top of the nail has a decorative, faceted head.

HARDY BENDING FORK

ROLL BAR ASSEMBLY

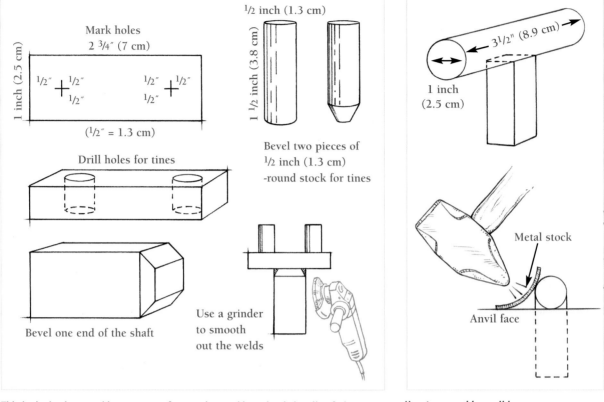

This is the basic assemblage pattern of parts when making a hardy bending fork.

How to assemble a roll bar.

Hardy Bending Fork

This tool will allow you to see the curves created during scroll forming as you are forging the iron. It allows the smith to do any bending process face up, instead of on its edge as when scrolls are formed on the horn or edge of the anvil.

You can make several bending forks. The distance between the pegs affects the radius of the curves.

Take a piece of plate steel, 1 x 2½ x ½ inches (2.5 x 6.4 x 1.3 cm) thick. Mark off the center lengthwise and ½ inch (1 cm) from each end. Center punch the cross marks and pilot drill the holes.

Change out your drill bit to ½ inch (1.3 cm) diameter and drill through the plate for both holes.

Cut two pieces of ½ inch (1.3 cm) -round stock,

1½ inches (3.8 cm) long. Grind a deep beveled edge on one end of each pin.

Tap the pins into the plate holes, bevel side meeting up with the bottom surface of each plate. The bevel will provided enough space to fill in with welding rod or wire and still retain a flush bottom and tight shoulders. Grind the underneath surface of the plate so that it is flush.

Cut a 2 inch (5.1 cm) piece of hardy square stock, making sure that it fits the hardy hole properly, and bevel all four sides of one end.

Secure the plate to your welding table, pins facing down or you can lay out pieces on their sides. Weld the hardy shaft to the center of the plate. Grind off any of the weld bead that flows outside of the beveled area to insure a flush seat in the anvil.

Roll Bar

I use this tool because my anvil does not have a step down area, (i.e., a table or chipping block). My anvil has a smooth flat face up until the neck of the horn.

Weld a piece of properly fitted shank stock to a piece of solid round bar that is slightly shorter then the width of your anvil face.

Use a round bar with any diameter of ¹/₂ inch (1.3 cm) or more. I made mine from a piece of 1 inch (2.5 cm) solid round stock. You will see how I use this tool in the project section of this book.

Monkey Tool

This is a finishing tool used to up the shoulders of tenoned stock. Its shape and size is determined by the shape and size of the stock that is being made into tenons.

For a round tenon monkey tool, use a 4 inch (10.7 cm) -long piece of solid round stock measuring 1 inch (2.5 cm) in diameter.

Find the center of one end and punch a mark into it (approximating will do). Secure it in the jaws of a drill press vise.

Pilot a small 1 inch (2.5 cm) long hole down the center of the stock. Replace the drill bit, sized to the tenon diameter you want to finish. For example, if you are making ¹/₂ inch (1.3 cm) tenons, drill the hole in the monkey tool using a ¹/₂-inch (1.3 cm) tip drill bit. Drill this hole 1 inch (2.5 cm) down into the shaft.

Make a port hole in the side of the stock by center punching ³/₄ inch (1.9 cm) down from the end of the stock material. Your port hole should measure ¹/₈ inch (3 mm) and should pierce into the side of the tenon hole. The port hole provides a view of the red hot tenon being driven into the main hole, and it also allows heat and fire scale an exit in addition to the tenon hole opening.

In order to work correctly, a monkey tool must match the tenons you have made—not only in

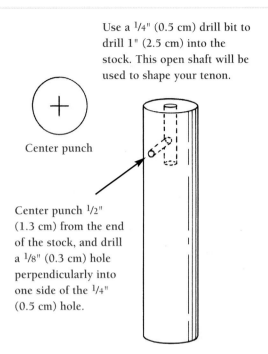

Use a ¹/₄" (0.5 cm) drill bit to drill 1" (2.5 cm) into the stock. This open shaft will be used to shape your tenon.

Center punch

Center punch ¹/₂" (1.3 cm) from the end of the stock, and drill a ¹/₈" (0.3 cm) hole perpendicularly into one side of the ¹/₄" (0.5 cm) hole.

The open shaft of the monkey tool must match the diameter and be at least as long as the tenon you are forming.

diameter, but also in length. It is okay to use the tool on tenons shorter than the monkey tool shaft, but if the tenon is longer, the function of dressing the shoulder of the tenon will not be achieved. To successfully finish a tenon, after being completely driven into the monkey tool shaft, its shoulder should rest against the flat surface of the monkey tool.

—◦◦◦—

I have many hardy tools for my anvil and the only ones that have a single position shaft are the hot cut and cold cut. They are made to fit one way to ensure a secure fit. I have marked them to help avoid jamming them in the wrong direction. All of my other hardy tools have shafts that can be inserted universally.

—◦◦◦—

Adjustable Twisting Wrench

I have seen several styles of twisting wrenches, but I prefer using an adjustable wrench and welding an additional handle that extends opposite of the existing handle. An adjustable wrench provides many advantages over a twisting bar wrench, the most obvious being that since it is adjustable, the number of twisting wrenches you will need to make is significantly reduced.

A twisting bar can only be used for one or two stock sizes—that adds up to a lot of wrenches. I have two adjustable twisting wrenches: one is for smaller stock (up to $1/2$ inch [1.3 cm] in diameter) and one for larger stock ($1/2$ inch to 1 inch [1.3 to 2.5 cm] in diameter). The design for a twisting bar that doesn't require welding is in the first section of this chapter.

You can use any type of adjustable wrench for this project; they are available at most flea markets. Just make sure that the jaws of the wrench are functioning, and that the threaded shaft of the tool is working.

Minimal rust can be removed with heat and a liquid solvent, so even if it appears to be "frozen," a rusted wrench may be salvageable.

Using the forging techniques you have practiced and learned, forge any kind of handle you want—just make sure that the secondary handle is the same length as the primary handle. Remember that if you like to hang your tools from hooks, forge a loop, ring, or scroll on the end of your handle.

Weld the new handle to the top of the wrench. Be sure to bevel the handle before attaching—this will provide more fill room for the welding rod or wire.

Pritchel Plate

This tool will help you in punching and drifting holes that are smaller than the size of the pritchel hole on your anvil. Appropriate sized holes reduce the distortion of the metal stock that is being drifted. The plate is large enough to sit on the anvil face, over the pritchel or hardy hole, but it is still considered a hand tool.

Get a piece of 10 x $3^{1/2}$ x $1/2$ inch (25.4 x 8.9 x 1.3 cm) -thick steel plate and torch cut a 4 inch (10 cm) handle.

Using a variety of bit sizes, drill a series of holes into the plate, but do not overcrowd the surface. Leave a minimum of 1 inch (2.5 cm) between the holes. The series of holes in my pritchel plate are sized between $1/4$ to $1/2$ inch (6 mm to 1.3 cm) in diameter.

After you have drilled the holes, use a grinder to smooth the top and bottom of the plate. I use a countersink bit in my drill press to bevel the holes just a little on both sides. This helps to keep anything from sticking to the plate when you are driving the drift into the hole.

To help identify the holes, it's a good idea to mark the diameters of the holes with numbered stamps. Drill a hole in the handle for hanging.

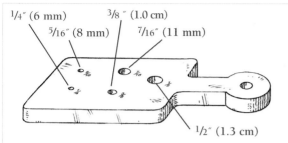

1/4" (6 mm)   3/8 " (1.0 cm)
5/16" (8 mm)   7/16" (11 mm)

1/2" (1.3 cm)

Punching over the pritchel plate.

Handheld Bending Fork

The difference in bending forks is determined by the distance between the pegs.

Start with a plate of tool steel measuring 1½ x 5 x ½ inches (3.8 x 12.7 x 1.3 cm).

Using the diagram as a reference, cut out the two notches using a torch or plasma cutter.

Draw out the mass for the handle and include a ring if you wish, to hang the fork. The overall length should reach at least 15 inches (38.1 cm).

Dress the tines of the fork using a grinder and belt sander. The interior surface of the tines should have smooth, rounded surfaces so that they will not mar the hot stock material.

Make several of these forks with different spacing and peg heights.

PATTERN AND DRAW-OUT OF A HAND-HELD BENDING FORK

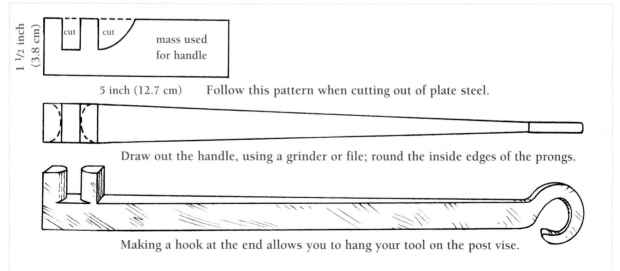

1 ½ inch (3.8 cm)

cut   cut   mass used for handle

5 inch (12.7 cm)   Follow this pattern when cutting out of plate steel.

Draw out the handle, using a grinder or file; round the inside edges of the prongs.

Making a hook at the end allows you to hang your tool on the post vise.

GUILLOTINE

The Guillotine is quite useful for the solo smith. Its design allows you to change out top and bottom dies—everything from rounded fullers to decorative ridges. Its design also accommodates larger diameter stock than the hardy spring fuller. A guillotine can be secured in a post vise or the hardy hole of the anvil.

Suggested Materials:

• Base: 3 x 4 inch (7.6 x 10.7 cm) plate steel
• Hardy: 3 inch (7.6 cm) of square stock that will fit the hardy hole of your anvil
• Brackets: 4 pieces of 1 x 1 x 3/8 inches (2.5 x 2.5 x 1.0 cm) angle iron
• One Set of Fuller Dies:
  Bottom: 1 x 4 x 1/2 inch (2.5 x 10.7 x 1.3 cm)
  Top: 3 x 4 x 1/2 inch (7.6 x 10.7 x 1.3 cm)

Clamp the plate down to the work table at the corners with a vise grip. This will ensure that the plate stays level and secure while welding the angle iron pieces in place.

   Place the angle iron vertically with the corners facing in and the two edges meeting the outer corners of the plate. I found it easier to lay out the whole thing before welding. Remember to use the top and bottom dies as spaces for the angle iron.

   Vise grip the top die stock and the four angle iron corners together. Place it on top of the plate base. Do all of the welding on the inside corners of the angle iron as it attaches to the base plate. The inner cross-section should remain flush and open to hold the bottom die in place.

PATTERN LAYOUT OF A GUILOTINE TOOL

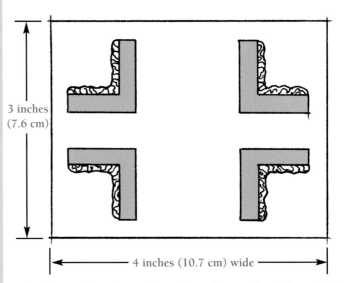

3 inches (7.6 cm)

4 inches (10.7 cm) wide

The blue marks indicate where the angle iron should be welded onto the plate. I suggest using 1″ x 1″ x 1/2″ (2.5 x 2.5 x 1.3 cm) angle iron, so the width is 1/4″ (6 mm).

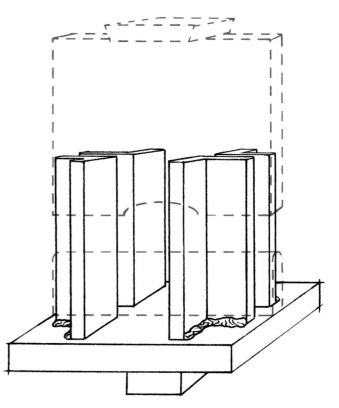

After the welding is complete, remove the clamps and top die. The die stock should be able to fit nicely into the grooves of the brackets. If the heat of the welding has caused the fit to be snug, use a grinder with a flap disc to narrow the lengthwise edges of the top and bottom dies so that they will drop into the bracket with ease.

The top die needs a striking surface. Weld a chuck of steel, 1¹/₂ x 1¹/₂ x ¹/₂ inches (3.8 x 3.8 x 1.3 cm) to the top edge.

Round off the bottom edge of the top die and the top edge of the bottom die.

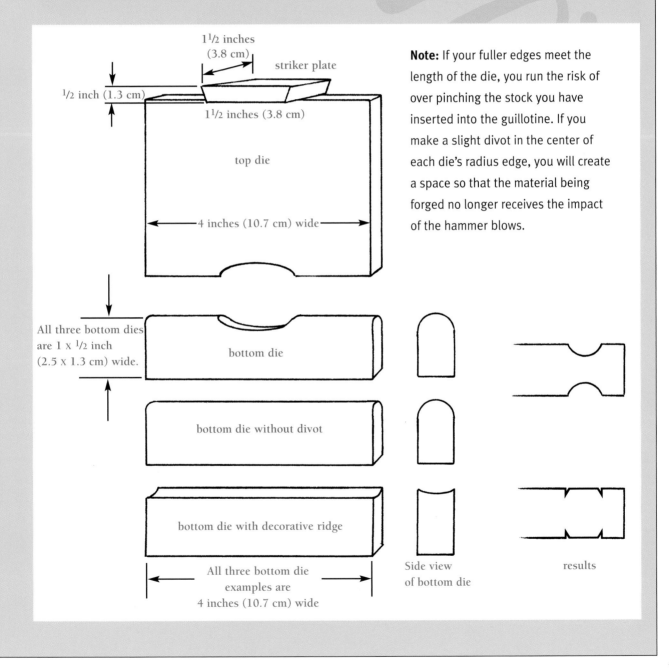

1¹/₂ inches (3.8 cm)
striker plate
¹/₂ inch (1.3 cm)
1¹/₂ inches (3.8 cm)
top die
4 inches (10.7 cm) wide

All three bottom dies are 1 x ¹/₂ inch (2.5 x 1.3 cm) wide.
bottom die
bottom die without divot
bottom die with decorative ridge

All three bottom die examples are 4 inches (10.7 cm) wide

Side view of bottom die

results

Note: If your fuller edges meet the length of the die, you run the risk of over pinching the stock you have inserted into the guillotine. If you make a slight divot in the center of each die's radius edge, you will create a space so that the material being forged no longer receives the impact of the hammer blows.

HOW TO FABRICATE
A METAL ANVIL STAND

A sand filled, truncated anvil stand has worked very well for me. It will require good welded seams to keep the sand inside. Use the base dimensions of your anvil and the distance from your knuckles to the floor to determine the overall dimensions of the stand.

To make the floater plate, follow the curve of the anvil's foot and make curved brackets. This will keep your anvil stationary on the floater plate.

The top perimeter measurements of the four sides of the stand should be slightly larger than the dimensions of the floating top plate. For example: A top plate measuring 6 1/2 x 9 1/2 inches (16.5 x 24.13 cm) will need a stand perimeter measurement of 6 3/4 x 9 3/4 inches (17.1 x 24.8 cm) to be able to rest inside.

To create an outward angled stand, the bottom edges of the stand should be only about 1 1/2 inches (4 cm) longer than the top edges of the stand. If the angle is too much, the base will be too wide, which will prevent you from getting your feet up and close. This will cause your lower back to bend, creating a domino effect of bad posture and sore muscles. The bottom plate that gets welded on can be the exact same outside perimeter as the four sided bottom opening, or it can be slightly larger than the bottom perimeter, creating a foot around the base.

When welding, the walls and base should have a continuous bead or seam so that the tiny grains of sand won't spill out with each hammer blow.

FABRICATING AN ANVIL STAND

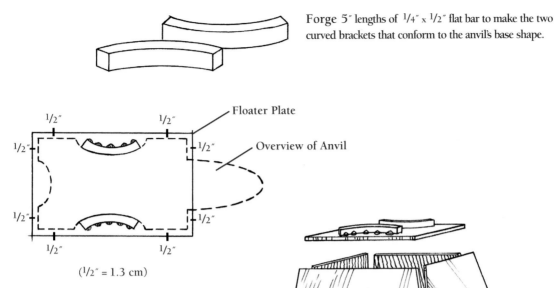

Forge 5″ lengths of ¹/₄″ x ¹/₂″ flat bar to make the two curved brackets that conform to the anvil's base shape.

Floater Plate

Overview of Anvil

(¹/₂″ = 1.3 cm)

Stick weld the brackets onto the floater plate so that they follow the inside curved radius of your anvil's base shape.

The brackets should be set so that they are not tight—you should be able to slip the anvil into place with ease.

Weld the inside radius of the bracket curves, which is outside of where the anvil sits on the plate. Otherwise, your anvil will be resting on the bracket welds.

To determine the height of the anvil stand: Obtain the measurement from your knuckles to the floor and subtract the height of the anvil.

Your stand will consist of two equal sets of walls—one set to match the short sides of the floater plate and one set for the long sides of the floater plate.

The wall should be constructed from ³/₁₆″ or ¹/₂″ (4.8 mm or 1.3 mm) plate.

Make sure that the top of each wall is ¹/₈″ (3 mm) longer than the floater plate measurement.

HEAT TREATMENT COLOR CHART

Color	Fahrenheit	Celsius
Pale Yellow	420°	216°
Straw Yellow	460°	238°
Dark Yellow	480°	249°
Dark Brown	510°	266°
Purple	540°	282°
Dark Purple	550°	288°
Blue	560°	293°
Dark Blue	570°	299°
Pale Blue	590°	310°
Grey	630°	332°

Working with High Carbon Tool Steel

Tool steel is a type of high carbon steel whose characteristics—toughness, resistance to abrasion and deformation, and ability to maintain a cutting edge—making it an excellent material for creating tools.

Carbon steel tools can be hardened to a depth of one ¼ inch (6 mm). Carbon steel has a granular structure that should not be heated higher than a bright red or light orange color temperature, less it will become weak and brittle. High carbon steels contain anywhere from 0.45 to 1.70 percent carbon. The higher the percentage of carbon, the harder a piece of steel may be tempered and the more difficult it becomes to weld.

FORGING HIGH CARBON STEEL

Always heat high carbon steel in a clean, coke fire. As with all heating, it is important to maintain a controlled forge fire—if you attempt to heat the material too rapidly, unequal expansion of the material molecules may occur as the outside heats faster than the inside of the material, which results in internal flaws and weakness.

Never heat tool steel above a bright red or light orange heat. Higher temperatures will change the granular structure—it will become large and weak, rather than condensed and strong.

Do not forge high carbon steel when it has not reached the appropriate color temperature—your stock material will crack and strain.

When forging high carbon steel, it is important to use heavy hammering to reduce the grain size, resulting in a refined piece of tool steel.

ANNEALING HIGH CARBON STEEL

Annealing is the process of cooling the steel before it is hardened and tempered. Annealing occurs after a project has been forged, and it allows the metal material to self-correct any minor internal strains that may have occurred during the heating and hammering process. In order to anneal, the metal should be heated to a dark red color temperature and then embedded into a bucket packed with sand, unused kitty litter, or refractory cloth—materials that will slow the cooling process but not melt. The container should be put in a draft-free room and allowed to cool off very slowly overnight.

HARDENING AND TEMPERING TOOL STEEL

After tools are forged and annealed, the working surfaces of the tools should be hardened and tempered. It is important to recognize that in addition to the carbon content affecting the potential hardness of a material, rapid cooling off also increases the hardness of steel, leading to a strained piece of metal.

If high carbon steel is heated to a dark red color temperature and quenched in water, it will become hard and brittle, so the material must be tempered. Tempering is the process of softening metal. It reduces the hardness a little, but removes the brittleness a lot. In order to temper tool steel, the material should be reheated to a critical temperature. The amount of tempering that occurs depends upon the temperature to which the material was reheated.

High carbon steels should be tempered to specific tempering color temperatures—the heat of the metal must surpass a critical temperature point. Tempering occurs from 350°F to 1350°F (180°C to 680°C), depending upon the type of steel used and the hardness desired. (Use the chart shown on opposite page to determine the appropriate color indicators for carbon steel.)

HARDENING

Reheat the tool to a red color temperature or slightly above the point where it becomes non-magnetic. This is called the Curie Point. Dip it into your quench bucket, moving it up and down, back and forth, side to side—this movement helps it cool as fast as possible.

The steel is now at its maximum hardness, but the material is very brittle.

TEMPERING

Use a file, steel wheel, or another abrasive to clean and polish the tool surface areas that will be making contact with your stock materials. This is important because it will allow for you to see the tempering color appearance. Clean the surrounding areas as well. For example, chisels and punches should be cleaned 2 to 3 inches (5.1 to 7.6 cm) from the cutting edge.

Using a torch or the outer area of the forge, heat up the unclean area of the tool, just below the cleaned and polished surface. As the heat transfers through the tool, you will notice the color changing. When the "working area" of the tool has reached its proper tempering color, quench the tool in water.

—∞—

One of the best tool gathering events I have ever attended occurs annually in Troy, Ohio. Every September, SOFA (Southern Ohio Forge and Anvil) hosts an annual conference that includes demonstrations and a gigantic tailgate sales area. You will be able to find everything from hot cuts to trip hammers, and you will also meet some very fun and knowledgeable people.

—∞—

3 Getting in the Groove

We can do it! This is it! You are now ready to employ your skills and make items that can be used in your smithy, home, and garden that will be graciously accepted as gifts by your friends and family.

CHAPTER EIGHT

PROJECTS

The projects in this chapter have been grouped according to skill level—beginner, intermediate, and advanced. Take my word, and start from the beginning. There is no substitute for accomplishing the easier ones before forging ahead to the more difficult projects. I guarantee that when you make your first usable drive hook, you will think about a career as the happy hook maker. This chapter will test your new-found skills, and if at first you do not succeed, try, try again. I did.

Drive Hook, J-Hook, and S-Hook

SKILL LEVEL: Easy

SKILLS USED: Tapering (page 69), Scrolling (page 75), Twisting (page 82), and Punching (page 88)

SUGGESTED MATERIAL:

Drive Hook: $^1/_4$ inch (0.6 cm) –square stock

J Hook: $^1/_4$ inch or $^3/_8$ inch (0.6 or 1 cm) –round or –square stock

S Hook: $^1/_4$ inch or $^3/_8$ inch (0.6 or 1 cm) –round or –square stock

Making hooks is the surest way to keep you motivated while learning this craft. They are fairly quick and easy to make, they employ several critical skills that need to be mastered, and they are just about the handiest item for a smithy to make and perfect for gift giving.

Drive Hook

This is the simplest hook that can be forged—it does not require a hole for a nail or screw. The tapered end is bent 90 degrees from the hook, and it forms the nail that is driven into the wood, therefore, the taper should be very pointy.

Use $^1/_4$-inch (0.6 cm) -square stock. Start by forging a ribbon taper on one end of the material.

This drive hook uses square stock for a decorative twist.

Quenching the tip before shaping the hook will help keep the shape of the scroll.

After you have forged a ribbon taper, scroll the tip. Reheat the stock and quench the scroll tip. Use the horn of the anvil to shape this end of the stock into the letter J. Remember to have the scroll tip up when making the J.

Hot cut about 2 inches (5.1 cm) away from the curve and taper the end into a nice sharp point.

Reheat the tapered end, place the taper off the far edge of the anvil, scrolled tip facing upwards, and strike the taper down into a 90 degree bend.

> ## Trick of the Trade
> Use long parent stock to work with instead of cutting each hook length before forging.

J-Hook

This hook will need a hole punched in it. The finial of the hook can be plain or decorative, and the stock can be round or square. Feel free to experiment with different lengths of material. You can opt to use already cut pieces or work from parent stock—whichever works better for you.

To make the top end of the hook that will have the hole punched, place the heated stock on the close edge of the anvil and hammer, with the J-shape facing downward. Your blows should be half on and half off the edge of the anvil. This will thin down just the tip of the stock, creating a little shoulder.

To make a leaf tip, simply taper the tip before flattening. If the tip is left undressed, the flattening process will make a rounded shape. Punch a hole through the enlarged area.

If you are using square stock, make a ribbon taper on the other end. If you use round stock, forge a round taper on the other end. Scroll the tip.

Reheat and quench the scrolled tip. Shape the stock into a hook using the anvil horn.

Remember, it is much easier to punch the stock before the hook is made. Make the finial and hole before cutting from the parent stock, or if you are using cut stock, don't form the J-hook until the opposite end has been spread and punched.

Go ahead and try forging the hook in reverse order. Learning what sequence works best for you is an early lesson in blacksmithing. All of the information remains the same even though the steps to creating a project can sometimes be reversed.

S-Hook

The S-hook uses the very same forming techniques as the drive and J-hooks.

Dress and scroll both tips of the stock, but make sure that the dressed ends are quenched before the scrolls are curled.

Remember that the scrolls should be formed opposite of each other. The first scroll tip should be facing upward when you begin hammering down on the second scroll tip.

If you forget to scroll in the opposing direction and end up making a C-hook, simply reheat the C in the forge. Quench just less than one half of the hook and insert the cooled portion into the vise jaws. To create an S-hook, use a twisting wrench to rotate the heated portion 180 degrees.

For an additional challenge, use square stock and bend the S-hook on the diamond. This means that you do all the forming while the stock is rotated 45 degrees, resting on one ridge or corner of the stock, rather than sitting flat on the anvil surface.

This square-stock S-hook is accented by a decorative twist in the middle.

How about an S-hook that incorporates on the diamond forming and a twist? Your skills will improve as long as you keep challenging yourself.

Hanging rods can be used to suspend plants from the ceiling or from wall mount hooks. Remember that the shaft of the hook does not have to be straight—I like very organic and curly shapes. Plant hangers can be as unique as you want.

Stakes for Glass Vessels

SKILL LEVEL: Easy
SKILLS USED: Tapering (page 69), Scrolling (page 75), and Wrapping (page 103)
SUGGESTED MATERIAL: 1/4 inch, 3/8 inch, or 1/2 inch (0.6, 1.9, or 1.3 cm) –round stock

This project has a very simple design and is a great gift idea for your friends and family. The stakes go into the ground, and the wrapped end holds the glass vessel. The glass can then be filled with oil and wick, a votive candle, flowers, or it can be used to hold a can of your favorite beverage.

A wide variety of inexpensive glass vessels can be found in most chain stores. The most important design element for the vessel is that it has an edged lip, which allows for the iron wrap to hold the glass in place. The larger the glass vessel, the bigger the stock size needs to be. The corkscrew bottom end helps keep the stake upright and secure in the ground.

The height of the stakes will vary depending upon the stock lengths you use. One use for outdoor party night-lights is to forge stakes of varying heights and stagger them throughout your yard.

I have found that a little bit of sand in the bottom of each vessel helps prevent melted wax from sticking to the glass. The glass will protect your candle flame from the wind, but use caution and make sure the glass is cool before picking it up.

Decorative scrolls can be added to the top section. The stakes can also be painted any color you wish and any type of spray paint may be used. I have painted some of mine green so that they are hidden among the landscape, which makes the vessels appear to be floating among the lilies.

I've used variations of this design to make garden stakes that hold clay pots for flowers and clay trays for birdseed. The different uses are abundant.

The only forging that occurs is on the tip of the stock that will hold the vessel, and on the taper at the opposite end, which is driven into the ground.

The rest of work is simply heating and adjusting the wrapping to securely hold your container.

Door Pull

SKILL LEVEL: Intermediate

SKILLS USED: Fullering (page 68), Tapering (page 69), Chisel Work (page 86), Punch and Drift (page 87), and Scrolling (page 75)

SUGGESTED MATERIAL: 16 inch (40.6 cm) piece of 1 inch x ⅛ inch (2.5 x 0.3 cm) flat stock

Nothing says welcome more than a hand-forged door pull on your front door. This project combines traditional elements, but as you progress in your skill level, you can make them as fun as your personality dictates.

1. Fuller 4 inches (10.7 cm) down from the tip on one end and fuller 1 inch (2.5 cm) down from the opposite end.

2. Divide the 4 inch (10.7 cm) end section in half lengthwise, leaving 1 inch (2.5 cm) uncut from the fuller.

3. Chisel cut through the marked portion using a copper plate to protect the anvil face.

4. Draw out one end to a taper. Mark the length of the first taper on the anvil before drawing out the second taper. Punch and drift the mass that is between the fuller and the cut line. This will be one of the areas that will secure the door pull with a nail or screw.

5. Separate the tines on the anvil horn.

6. Scroll each tine opposite to whatever radius you want.

7. Forge a long taper in the center section. This taper gives your door pull a nice grip and visual appearance.

8. To dress the other end of the door pull, which was fullered earlier, taper the 1 inch (2.5 cm) section to a single point.

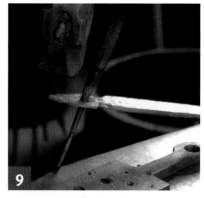

9. Punch and drift a hole through the point, close to the fuller. This will be the second point of attachment to the door.

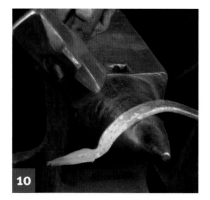

10. Form the handle over the horn.

11. Flatten the taper so that it sits flush on the face of the anvil.

12. Flatten the scrolled end so that it is level with the tapered end.

If this piece is used as an outdoor handle, wire brush the piece well, reheat it until hot to the touch, and apply wax mixture (see page 165) to seal the ironwork.

Gate Pull

SKILL LEVEL: Intermediate

SKILLS USED: Tapering (page 69), Near Side and Far Side Hammering (page 62), Twisting (page 82), Bending (page 73), and Punch and Drift (page 87)

SUGGESTED MATERIAL: 6 inch (15.2 cm) piece of 3/8 inch (1 cm) –square stock

These are smaller versions of the door pull and can be used for outside gates, as well as for kitchen and bath cabinet pulls.

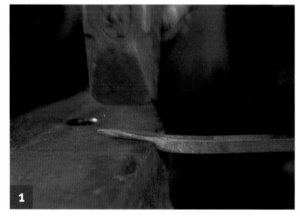

1. Taper ends of the stock and hammer half-face over the near edge of the anvil to make leaves.

2. Punch and drift small holes in each of the leaf finials.

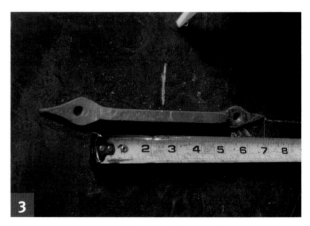

3. Use soapstone to mark the center of the stock between the leaves, then center punch.

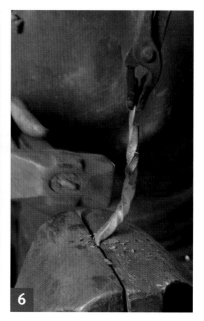

4. Heat one end and secure it in the vise before twisting. Reheat the other end. Make sure to quench the side that has already been twisted to prevent marring while in the jaws of the vise.

5. Secure the cooled end in the vise and twist the metal in the opposite direction, repeating the same twist revolution as the first.

6. Heat one end and secure it in the vise at the leaf end. Hammer outward to make a curve.

7. Reheat the other end, secure it in the vise, and make a curve that mirrors the first curve.

8. Reheat both ends and flatten them on the anvil face so that they will lay flush on a flat mounting surface.

Leaf Letter Opener

SKILL LEVEL: Intermediate

SKILLS USED: Tapering (page 69), Drawing Out (page 69), and Spreading (page 71)

SUGGESTED MATERIAL: 5 inch (12.7 cm) piece of $^1/_2$ inch (1.3 cm) –round stock

With the advent of electronic mailing taking precedence, one would think that a letter opener as a tool is obsolete. *Au Contraire…* Having a handmade letter opener is just as nice as receiving a handwritten letter.

1. To make the leaf finial, taper the tip of the stock. To form the stem leading to the leaf, extend the taper 1" (2.5 cm) past the far edge of the anvil and apply half hammer blows.

2. Place the tip on the near edge of the anvil and flatten. Rotate the hammer and use the cross peen to form the leaf shape.

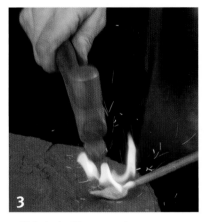

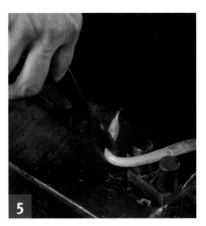

3. Sink the leaf into a wooden stump or a swage block.

4. To make the blade of the letter opener, taper and draw out the end, and flatten it. Remember, letter opener blades need to be fairly thin. You can curve the blade slightly or keep it straight.

5. Use your scroll tongs and bending fork to bring the leaf back around to the blade.

6. Use a brass bristle brush to color the leaf and wax-seal the warm metal.

7. The blade can be finished to your desired sharpness. Secure the opener in your vise and use a file to finish the edges of the blade.

Wall Mount Hook and Dinner Bell

SKILL LEVEL: Intermediate

SKILLS USED: Tapering (page 69), Bending (page 73), Scrolling (page 75), Chisel (page 86), and Punch and Drift (page 87)

SUGGESTED MATERIAL:

Wall Mount Hook: 10 inch (25.4 cm) length of 3/8 inch (1 cm) –round stock

Dinner Bell Triangle: 34 1/2 inch (87.6 cm) length of 1/2 inch (1.3 cm) –round stock

Dinner Bell Strike: 10 inch (25.4 cm) length of 1/2 inch (1.3 cm) –round stock

As with most projects, when creating a larger hook, a larger diameter of stock should be used. Wall mount hooks are perfect for hanging plants, bird feeders, dinner bells, or chimes. Small versions of this project can be used to hold curtain rods.

The Dinner Bell is a perfect housewarming gift, whether you live in the country or not. It tells you friends they can call you anything … just not late for dinner!

WALL MOUNT HOOK

1. Taper and scroll both ends of the stock. Use the horn or a bending fork to form the scrolls.

2. Punch two holes about 2 inches (5.1 cm) apart near one end of the stock.

3. Heat and curl the other end of the stock to form an arch.

DINNER BELL

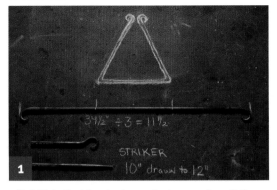

1. To initiate the triangle, draw out a taper and scroll the tip of both ends of the stock. Measure the length of the rod, divide by three, and use a chisel to mark the three separate sections.

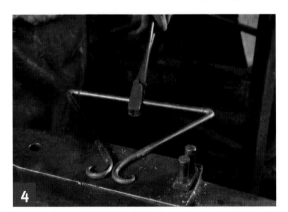

2. Secure one end of the stock in your vise. Using a torch to create an isolate heat on the first mark, closest to the vise, make the first bend to create a 120 degree angle.

3. Heat and bend the second mark, creating another 120 degree angle which forms the triangle.

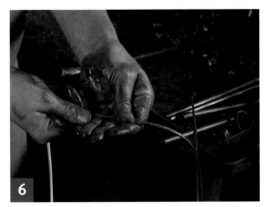

4. Heat the scroll tips and straighten out any distortions that may have occurred when bending the triangle.

5. To forge the striker, make a simple tapered eye hook on one end of the stock material. The eye hook should not be completely closed. Allow enough room for the strike to hang from the bottom of the dinner bell.

6. Use a leather cord to hang the dinner bell from the wall hook. Spray an oil-based lubricant on your dirty hands and rub it into the cord.

Camping Pot Rack

SKILL LEVEL: Intermediate

SKILLS USED: Tapering (page 69), Upsetting (page 72), Punch and Drift (page 87), and Bending (page 73)

SUGGESTED MATERIAL:

Legs: Two 36 inch (0.9 m) pieces of ¹/₂ inch (1.3 cm) –round stock

Crossbar: 20 inch (51 cm) piece of ³/₈ inch (1 cm) –round stock

Hooks: 5 inch (13 cm) pieces of ¹/₈ inch (0.3 cm) –round stock

Those that know and love camping will take extra pride in using these items while sleeping under the stars. They can also be used as *object d'art* in any garden.

1. Make an eye hook on one end of the stock, slightly larger than the crossbar stock diameter. Heat the other end of the material and form a hook. The quantity of hooks is your choice.

2. Next, form the legs of the stand. Heat and taper one end of each leg. Quench or let cool. Then heat and upset the opposing ends of the material.

3. Punch and drift a 3/8 inch (1 cm) hole 1 1/2 inches (3.8 cm) down from the upset ends.

4. To forge the cross bar, bend one end of the 3/8 inch (1 cm) -round stock into a rounded curve.

5. Upset the opposite end of the crossbar and form a rivet head. This will prevent the bar from slipping out of the legs once the rack is assembled.

ASSEMBLAGE:

When you are ready to put the camp pot rack into use, make sure to follow these steps.

1. Drive one vertical bar into the ground.

2. Starting with the curved end, slip the cross bar through the leg hole.

3. Slip all of the hooks onto the cross bar.

4. Visually estimate the placement of the second vertical bar.

5. Slip the second leg onto the curved end of the crossbar before driving the leg into the ground.

6. Hang your cooking gear on the hooks.

Scroll Candle Holder

SKILL LEVEL: Intermediate

SKILLS USED: Upsetting (page 72), Punch and Drift (page 87), Scrolling (page 75), Riveting (page 99), Bending (page 73), Guillotine (page 116), and Hot Cut (page 109)

SUGGESTED MATERIAL: 16 inch (40.6 cm) piece of 1¹/₂ x ¹/₄ inch (3.8 x 0.6 cm) –flat stock

This candle holder is made from thick-gauge material. Its thickness may be harder to work with, but not impossible. The finished product can stand alone or as a pair. With slight variations in length and stock width, you can create a nice arrangement for your dining table or mantel.

Forming the Candle Cup involves using the guillotine technique, which you have learned, but in this project we are using pipe. Pipe moves the same way as solid stock but you need to be gentle when initially working the material. You do not want to collapse the pipe on its edge—you want to fuller or pinch the pipe's radius gradually. Therefore, when starting the fullering of the pipe, make sure that you rotate the pipe with each hammer blow until you have indented a complete circle.

1. Upset both ends of the flat stock. Punch and drift a ³/₈ inch (1 cm) hole 7 inches (17.8 cm) down from the one of the upsetted ends.

> ### ➤➤ SAFETY TIP
>
> Forging pipe is different than forging solid stock. Trap the hot air that will travel through the pipe by blocking the back end with wadded newspaper. This will help keep the parent stock cool.

2. Scroll the end nearest to the hole.

3. Making the **Candle Cup:** Once you have established the fuller mark around the radius of the pipe, your hammer blows can become more aggressive. Fuller or pinch the section until it closes.

4. Heat the cup and flare the lip by placing it on the horn tip and using a hammer. Notice the angle of the cup needed to flare the rim.

5. Shape the shoulder of the cup before cutting it off the parent pipe stock.

6. You will need to use tongs to heat and dress the stem until it fits through the hole you made in the flat stock.

7. Heat the candle cup stem and quench the cup before placing it upside down on the anvil. Lay the flat stock upside down, aligning the hole with the stem. Compress the stem and form a rivet.

8. Heat the area that has the rivet. Using the hardy bending fork and handheld bending fork, tweak and shape the curl.

9. Heat the other end of the scroll base, and using your hardy bending fork and tongs, bend a slight radius following the scroll arch.

10. The last bending is to flip the upset edge and form the opposite curl. This gives your piece a graceful look, helps to level the candle holder, and protects the table surface on which it will sit.

Camping Tripod

SKILL LEVEL: Intermediate

SKILLS USED: Tapering (page 69) and Bending (page 73)

SUGGESTED MATERIAL:

Tripod Legs: Three 36 inch (0.9 cm) lengths of ½ inch (1.3 cm) –round stock

S-Hook: 12 inch (30.9 cm) length of ¼ inch (0.6 cm) –round stock

S-Hook: 6 inch (15.2 cm) length of ¼ inch (0.6 cm) –round stock

Ring: 9 inch (22.9 cm) length of ½ inch (1.3 cm) –round stock

This project will evoke memories of your scouting days. You will need to make three legs, a ring, and two S-hooks to construct your new camping pot. To support your steaming caldron of beans and weenies, the stakes need to be driven securely into the dirt.

TRIPOD LEGS

1. Heat the stock materials to a bright orange color temperature and taper the end of each of the three pieces. Cool the ends. The length of the tapers can be short or long, but they must come to a sharp point so that they can be securely driven into the ground.

2. Heat the opposite ends and hammer out a 3½ inch (8.9 cm) long ribbon taper on each of the three lengths. Use the horn to initiate the offset eye.

3. Apply back blows to curl the ribbon taper and form an offset closed eye, making sure the opening is large enough for your ring material to slip through.

RING

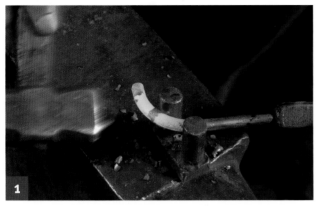

1. Form a ring using the round stock material and a hardy fork. The ring does not need to be forge welded closed, so you do not need to scarf the ends of the material. However, if you want the rings to have a smooth closure, slightly bevel each end in opposite directions so that the edges will line up and form an angled closure. Notice that the end of the material has not been scarfed since the ring will not be forge welded.

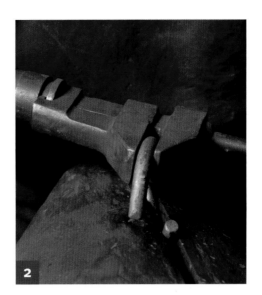

2. Open the ring after it has been secured in your vise. The ring should be inserted half way into the vise, with the ring opening level to the vise jaws. It is important to open the ring by twisting rather than spreading. The shape of the ring will not be distorted if you twist it open. Use your twisting wrench by attaching it to the top section of the exposed ring, with the opening just wide enough to reed the three tapered eyes onto the ring.

3. Make sure the offset eyes are facing the same direction as they are fed onto the ring.

S-HOOKS

Make two S-hooks, each a different length to allow for height adjustments of a kettle or cauldron. The hooks can be decorative or plain. If you decide to leave them plain, dress the tips with a little taper.

The tripod works best when it is set up on ground, not asphalt. To be stable and securely hold the cooking vessel, the tripod needs to be sunken into the dirt.

When setting it up, let the tripod find its own position, with the ring almost vertical and one tripod leg standing a bit higher than the other two.

Forge Fire Tools

SKILL LEVEL: Intermediate

SKILLS USED: Tapering (page 69), Drawing Out (page 69),
Twisting (page 82), Spreading (page 71),
Scrolling (page 75), and Wrapping (page 103)

SUGGESTED MATERIAL:

Flux Spoon: 18 inch (45.7 cm) length of 3/8 inch
                   (1 cm) –round stock

Rake: 30 inch (76.2 cm) length of 1/2 inch
                   (1 cm) –round stock

Water Can Holder: 28 inch (71 cm) length of 1/2 inch
                   (1 cm) –square stock and an empty
                   soup can

One of the joys of blacksmithing is the ability to make
your own tools. Some of these projects can be used for
a wood burning fireplace, as well as the coal forge.

Trick of the Trade

To make the forge fire tools easier projects,
make a simple handle such as a cable twist,
fish tail scroll, or hook handle.

FLUX SPOON

A long-handled flux spoon safely allows you to apply flux to hot metal during the forge welding process.

1. Upset one end of the stock to build up mass for the bowl of the spoon.

2. Place the upset tip 1 inch (2.5 cm) past the far side of the anvil, and use half hammer blows to taper down the neck. This will provide a gentle transition between the spoon shaft and the bowl.

3. Flatten and spread the spoon bowl using the cross peen of the hammer.

4. Sink the spoon into a swage block or a wood stump.

5. To forge the spoon handle, taper the other end of the material.

6. Heat a section of stock 6 to 8 inches (15.2 to 20.32 cm) down from the taper so the metal can be bent back upon itself.

7. The tip should meet with the spoon shaft.

8. Make a long heat on the doubled-up portion of stock and secure it perpendicularly into the vise jaws. Remember that both the shaft and the tapered tip must be secured in the vise.

9. Insert a rod or pipe into the loop and begin twisting the metal so that it wraps around itself.

10. Reheat the area that was locked inside the vise, and use scroll tongs to shape the exposed tapered tip.

RAKE

This rake design incorporates a tip for poking and breaking up coal while tending the fire, along with a scoop to rake coal to the center of the fire pot.

To create the handle, I recommend a fish tail scroll. It is easy and provides a nice grip on any forge fire tool.

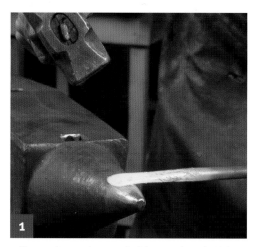

1. Heat and spread one end of the round stock. Using a cross peen hammer, apply your blows so that they radiate from the center out to the edges. This starts the fish tail scroll.

2. Heat 5 inches (12.7 cm) down from the scroll and loop the material back around.

3. Carry the scroll tip back to the main parent stock until it touches. Quench and let cool. The size of this loop should be gauged by the size of your hand.

4. To create the poker, taper 2 inches (5.1 cm) of stock into a point on the opposing end of the stock material. Do not make a thin taper—a sturdy point is needed to break up clumps of coal. Keep the line of the shaft, scoop, and tip point as linear as possible.

(continued)

5. Use a cross peen to spread a 3 to 4 inch (7.6 to 10.7 cm) section just above the taper. Spread the material in one direction away from the parent shaft.

6. Form the scoop around the horn, making a slight arch or curve. If you are left handed, the scoop should curl opposite of what is depicted in the photograph.

7. Bend back the poking tip so that it points perpendicular, 90 degrees from the shaft.

WATER CAN HOLDER

The handle of this tool is a simple scroll finished with a ribbon taper.
You know the drill, taper one end and scroll it.

1. Draw and flatten out enough material to go around three-quarters of the soup can. If you are unsure of the length, use a cloth tape measure around the can. Shape the tapered section to form an open-ended eye hook. The opening needs to be large enough to squeeze the can through.

2. Punch holes into one side of the bottom of the can. This will allow you to sprinkle from that side and pour from the other.

3. Squeeze the can into the eye hook. To create a spout, pinch the rim of the can.

BBQ Fork with Basket Weave Handle

SKILL LEVEL: Advanced

SKILLS USED: Forge Welding (page 93), Drawing Out (page 69), Twisting (page 82), Tapering (page 69), Spreading (page 71), and Chisel Work (page 86)

SUGGESTED MATERIAL:

Basket Weave:	Four 6 inch (15.2 cm) lengths of $\frac{1}{4}$ inch (0.6 cm) –round stock
Fork:	30 inches (76.2 cm) of $\frac{1}{2}$ inch (1.3 cm) –round stock

When was the last time you saw a perfect fork for a camp fire? They don't exist. So make your own, invite your friends to a cookout, and impress them with a truly functional cooking tool.

1. To make the basket weave, use the vise to hold the four pieces of stock material together so you can wrap each end with bailing wire.

2. Insert one end of the bundle into the fire, bring to a forge welding heat, making sure to apply flux about 1 inch (2.5 cm) from the tip of the bundle. Rotate the bundle during the heat so that all sides are being heated evenly.

3. Bring the bundle to the anvil and forge weld the ends together. The hammer blows should follow the square shape of the bundle. Do not hit it on the corner edge. Try to keep the bundle square shaped, which will help you when it comes time to twist.

4. Forge weld the other tip in the same way. If any bailing wire is still attached, remove it. This is uncommon though, because it usually melts in the forge or breaks away when the hammer blows are made.

5. Heat the entire piece to a yellow forging temperature. Brush off any remaining flux.

(continued)

6. Secure 1 inch (2.5 cm) into the vise jaws horizontally. Use a twisting wrench to twist the stock until it is tight.

7. The tighter the material is wound, the better the basket weave. This single direction tight twist is also called a cable twist. The cable twist can be used as a decorative element as is, but to make a basket weave, a few more steps need to be followed.

8. Use the jaws of the vise as a press to straighten the material.

9. If the basket weave is to be used as a handle or forge welded to another piece of stock, keep the twist as a cable twist until all other forging has been completed. To weld the basket weave to a longer piece of material, scarf one end of the cable twist and one end of the long piece of stock. Make sure to use the vise to straighten out any bends.

10. Reheat the cable twist to an even yellow color temperature. Place the shaft into the vise and secure a twisting wrench to the other end of the material.

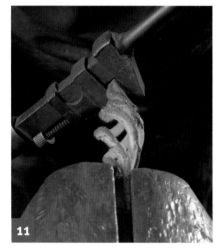

11. Begin a slow reverse twist to the material. The reverse twist motion causes the tight cable to open at its center and unwind. It is easy to distort the basket weave if you are not careful. Make sure that the wrench stays centered when reverse twisting.

12. There are always slight imperfections when opening the basket weave, but they can be adjusted by heating the weave and using scroll tongs to squeeze together any large spaces. Your goal is to make the weave pattern as uniform as possible.

13. Flatten the tip down 4 inches (10.7 cm) and chisel it in half lengthwise to form the fork end.

14. Taper the prongs to be very thin and pointed.

15. Mark the length of the first time before bending it back and tapering the second one.

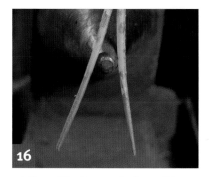

16. Spread the tines on the horn of the anvil.

17. Open and shape the crotch of the fork so the tines are 3 to 4 inches (7.6 to 10.7 cm) apart.

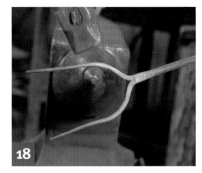

18. Bend the tines back, parallel with the fork shaft.

Door Knocker

SKILL LEVEL: Advanced

SKILLS USED: Tapering (page 69), Punching (page 88), and Forge Welding (page 93)

SUGGESTED MATERIAL:

Bracket: 10 inch (25.4 cm) length of ¹/₂ inch (1.3 cm) –round stock *

Ring: 12 inch (30.9 cm) length of ¹/₂ inch (1.3 cm) –round stock

Striker Plate: 2¹/₂ inch (6.4 cm) length of ¹/₂ inch (1.3 cm) –round stock *Because this part requires such a small piece of stock, add it to the length of the bracket material, and forge the striker plate first. Cut 12¹/₂ inches (31.7 cm) of ¹/₂ inch (1.3 cm) –round stock.

Door bells are so impersonal. Why not opt for the old-fashioned sound of an iron door knocker to say that friends have arrived? Door knockers can be created using numerous designs, as long as the three components are incorporated—a stationary bracket that holds a moving piece, which is then struck against another piece to make noise.

STRIKER PLATE

1. Forge a sharp and short taper on one end of the stock. Heat the stock 3 inches (7.6 cm) down from the tip of this taper and hot cut it off. Taper the other end of this short piece of material in the same fashion.

2. Once the material has cooled, drill out the holes. Punch a tiny hole in each end of the plate just deep enough to use a ¹/₈ inch (0.3 cm) drill bit. Countersink the holes.

BRACKET

1. With the remaining stock, form a leaf finial, taper to a point, and then taper a stem, leaving 1 inch (2.5 cm) of the tip for the leaf.

2. Use the cross peen to spread the leaf out, and chisel in the veins. Remember, leaves are very interpretational. Yours can be as large or as complex as you want. Reheat the stem and center punch 2 holes on the stock close to the leaf.

3. Sink the heated leaf, vein side down, into a divot on a wood stump. Do not use a swage block—metal on metal hammering will destroy the veining texture of the leaf.

4. Heat the other end of the stock, up to the holes, and make a very long and thin taper.

5. This will be the part of the bracket that wraps loosely around the ring.

6. Spread out 4 inches (10.7 cm) of the stock with a cross peen, making a ribbon taper in the center section.

RING

1. Heat and hammer texture the entire length of stock before shaping it into a ring. The texturing provides your ironwork with a finished look. There's nothing aesthetic about a smooth ring when the rest of the piece is hand-forged.

2. Scarf both ends, remembering to scarf the second end opposite of the first. When the ends of the ring meet, the scarfs should line up diagonally. Form the ring using the anvil horn or a hardy bending fork. Notice how the scarfed ends line up once the ring is formed.

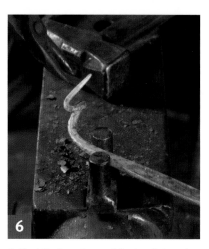

3. Heat the ring to a yellow-white forge welding color temperature. Before the color temperature is reached, apply flux to the scarfed area, and return the ring to the fire. The first hammer blows will be on the top flat edge of the ring.

4. After the impact has melded the ring, place it over the horn and forge weld the inner and outer edges. Remember that this two-part process of connecting the ends in a forge weld needs to happen very quickly. You may have to reheat the ring.

5. Let the ring cool and secure the ring in the vise with the forge-welded area facing upward. Use a file to clean up any lumps or ridges that may have resulted during the forge welding process. Secure the ring in the jaws of the vise.

6. Heat the long taper of the bracket, and use scroll tongs to form a tendril end. Bend the center of the long taper into a U shape, which will cradle the ring.

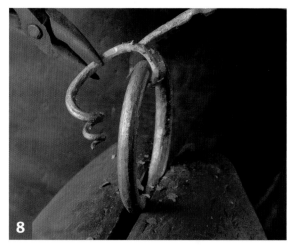

7. Feed the U shape through the ring, using tongs to make the wrap. Next, heat the area that begins the flattened ribbon taper and bend it back upon itself.

8. Use the scroll tongs to wrap the tendril end around the ring. The next heat should be as long as you can make it. The more material that is heated, the easier it will be to loosely wrap the bracket around the ring. Make sure that the knocker is operational—do not wrap it too tightly. If needed, use a gas torch to heat and adjust the wrap, tendril, and leaf. Make sure the punched holes of the bracket are properly aligned so that the ironwork can be mounted.

Gate Latch

SKILL LEVEL: Advanced

SKILLS USED: Fullering (page 68), Tapering (page 69), Upsetting (page 72), Hot Cutting (page 109), and Riveting (page 99)

SUGGESTED MATERIAL:

Brackets: Two lengths of 8 inch (20.32 cm) 1¹/₂ x ¹/₂ inch (3.8 x 1.3 cm) –flat stock

Handle: One 5 inch (13 cm) length of ³/₈ inch (1 cm) –round stock

Rivet: ³/₈ inch (1 cm) –round stock

A gate is only as good as the latch that secures it. This closure is both decorative and functional; a sturdy solution to some of life's little problems.

RIVET

1. Use the handle stock to make the rivet. Upset the tip of the 5 inch (12.7 cm) piece of round stock and form a rivet head. Form a tenon just below the upset mass, and hot cut the rivet off the metal stock.

BRACKETS

1

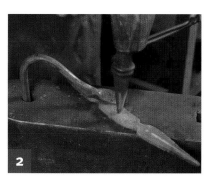

2

4

1. Fuller both ends of two pieces of flat stock material, approximately 1 ¹/₂ to 2 inches (3.8 to 5.1 cm) from each end, and taper the four ends to a flat point. Make sure to mark the length of the first taper on the anvil face to ensure that all of the tapers are uniformly sized.

2. Punch and drift a ³/₈ inch (1 cm) hole in the center of one of the brackets. The rivet will be attached here.

3. Punch and drift four mounting holes, one located on each of the tapered ends. The placement of the holes is optional, but try to avoid using the pinched and fullered areas.

4. Using a slit chisel, cut a three-sided tab in the center of the other bracket. Remember to flip the material over when cutting completely through, and use a copper plate on your anvil face.

(continued)

5. Remember to maintain a bright orange color temperature during the cutting process.

6. Pull the tab out to a 90 degree angle.

7. Clean up the edges of the tab and hole. The best way to clean the edges is with a file, while the piece is secured in the vise.

8. Reheat the tab and hammer it back down, with a piece of 3/8 inch (1 cm) –round stock between the bracket and the tab. This will give the tab the correct bend to hold the gate latch closed.

LATCH

1. Ribbon taper 2 inches (5.1 cm) of the 3/8 inch (1 cm) –round stock. The ribbon should be even throughout its entire length. Use back blows to form an offset eye with the opening a little bigger than the rivet stem you created earlier.

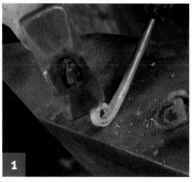
2. Heat and bend the other end of the stock to form the latch.

3. To assemble the latch, place the rivet upside down on the anvil face, and slide the latch and the bracket with the punched hole onto the rivet stem. The rivet stem should protrude about 1/4 inch (6 mm) from the bracket surface. If there is too much stem material, the underside of the bracket will have a bump that will prevent it from laying flush against the gate. The back of the bracket hole can be drifted at an angle to help create a slight countersink. When mounting the pieces to your wooden gate, make sure that the pointed end of the latch is facing downwards, and the brackets are spaced so that the latch easily catches the tab.

Pot and Utensil Rack

Not only is this rack perfect for the kitchen, it can also have a happy home hanging towels, coats, or the more than half-million keys that seem to follow your every move. I have one that I use to display dried herbs in my kitchen.

SKILL LEVEL: Advanced

SKILLS USED: Fullering (page 68), Tapering (page 69), Chisel Work (page 86), Punch and Drift (page 87), Riveting (page 99), Scrolling (page 75), and Bending (page 73)

SUGGESTED MATERIAL:

Bracket:	30 inch (76.2 cm) length of $1^{1}/_{2}$ x $^{3}/_{16}$ inch (3.8 cm x 4.8 mm) –flat stock
Center Hook:	6 inch (15 cm) length of $1^{1}/_{2}$ x $^{3}/_{16}$ inch (3.8 cm x 4.8 mm) –flat stock
Removable Hooks:	Two pieces of $6^{1}/_{2}$ x $^{1}/_{8}$ inch (16.5 x 0.3 cm) –flat stock and two pieces of $4^{1}/_{2}$ x $^{1}/_{8}$ inch (11.4 x 0.3 cm) –flat stock

BRACKET

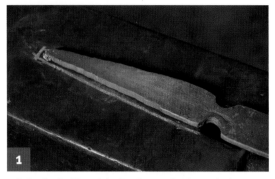

1. Fuller both sides of the bracket stock, about 4 inches (10.7 cm) down from the ends. Taper each end to a flat point, and mark the length of the first taper on your anvil face to help in making the second taper.

2. Draw the end to a long taper and chisel cut it in half down the center or band saw the cut. Be sure to leave 1 inch (2.5 cm) of the taper base next to the shoulder of the fuller uncut.

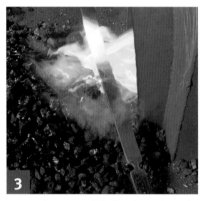

3. Heat the center of the bracket and punch a hole. This step can be done now, or after your tapers are split and scrolled.

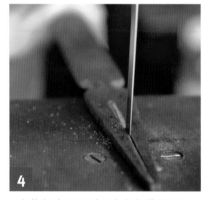

4. Split both tapered ends in half using a slit chisel or a band saw.

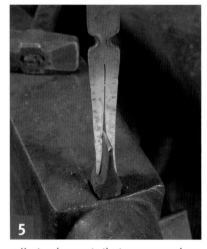

5. Heat and separate the two prongs using a hot cut to initiate the opening, and curl the tips outward.

6. After separating the two tongs, use the horn of the anvil and your scroll tongs to form the finial.

7. Continue to scroll the prongs until the desired look is achieved. The scrolls can be mirrored or asymmetrical, the choice is yours. Repeat this process on the other end of the stock.

CENTER HOOK

1. Fuller 2 inches (5.1 cm) from one end of the stock material.

2. Punch and drift a ¹/₄ inch (6 mm) hole for the ¹/₄ inch (6 mm) rivet near the fuller, on the side opposite the taper.

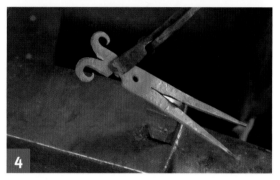

4. Another way to is to create two prongs on the opposite end of the stock. Use a band saw to split the metal in half, and taper the two sections.

3. You can create split-tapered prongs two different ways: On the 2 inch (5.1 cm) section of material, you can forge a flat-tapered point, using a chisel to split the taper in half. Use the edge of the anvil to separate the prongs before scrolling them outward.

5. Make sure to curl the tips of the tapers before forming them into the J-shaped double hook.

6. Use the anvil horn to form the J-shape double hooks.

7. Secure the hook in the vise so that you can spread the two J-hooks.

8. Use a rivet to attach the hook to the bracket, making sure that the hooks are curling forward when assembling.

9. Heat the middle section of the bracket and bend it into a slight arch. It may be necessary to secure a hardy bending fork into the vise, and use a handheld bending fork to get the curve just the way you you want it.

10. Once the piece has a nice curve to it, the scrolled ends need to be flattened out to fit flush against the wall.

11. Heat the ends of the bracket, and use the side of the anvil to make the angled bends.

REMOVABLE HOOKS

These removable and adjustable hooks are made from flat stock material and hang off the bracket either as a one-sided single hook, or as a two-sided double hook. Do not curl the tips of the hooks; this will allow them to be used with cookware and utensils that have small openings for hanging.

1. Slightly taper the ends of your stock material.

2. Wrap the heated metal around a piece of stock material the same size as the bracket stock size.

3. Curl the end to make a hook. If it is a double hook, make sure to curl the ends opposite each other.

Snake

SKILL LEVEL: Advanced

SKILLS USED: Tapering (page 69), Spreading (page 71),
Upsetting (page 72), and Chiseling (page 86)

SUGGESTED MATERIAL: 24 to 30 inch (62.2 to 76.2 cm) length
of 3/8 inch (1 cm) –round stock (a long
piece of parent stock keeps you from
having to use tongs)

Snakes are my favorite item to demonstrate. They incorporate many different forging skills and they do not take very long to make. Each one is different, and at the end of the process, when I dip the snake into the wax mixture, I tell the children in the audience that the hissing noise they hear is the snake coming to life!

Because there are quite a few multi-tasking steps, I would rate the snake head-making portion of this exercise as advanced. But, the more times you do the whole project, the better your snake heads will turn out. Don't be discouraged if your first few heads look more like common screwdrivers than reptiles.

1. First heat: This step creates the separation of the back of the head and the neck. Place 1 inch (2.5 cm) piece of stock material over the far edge of the anvil and use half hammer blows.

2. Rotate the stock by a quarter turn and repeat the half hammer blows. Keep the stock slightly angled towards the far edge and use the sharpest edge on your anvil's far edge, not the rounded edge used when making scrolls.

3. Draw down, from the head back, a 1 inch (2.5 cm) taper. This is the neck area. Break the corners and return to round.

4. Next heat—Place the head mass at the nearest edge of the anvil and flatten the tip just a little bit.

5. Rotate the snake head, and use the cross peen to spread the area closest to the taper. This forms the jaws of the snake.

6. Rotate the snake head a quarter turn, place it on the far edge of the anvil, and slightly taper the tip.

7. Heat the other end and forge a long skinny taper for the tail.

8. Bend the neck back and lower the head. This elevates the snake head from the the body.

9. Using the horn of the anvil or a hardy bending fork, shape the body of the snake into any form your want.

Rasp Asp

SKILL LEVEL: Advanced

SKILLS USED: Rolling, Tapering (page 69), Forge Welding (page 93), Chisel Work (page 86), Bending (page 73), and Punching (page 88)

SUGGESTED MATERIAL: An old farrier's file and a 1 inch (2.5 cm) piece of 3/8 inch (1 cm) –round stock

This project is rated advanced because the file is made from high carbon steel, which is harder to bend than low carbon steel.

The rolling can be laborious and keeping the seam running straight is difficult in the beginning. The key to a good rasp asp is to do all of the forming when the metal is yellow hot and to limit the number of hammer blows that directly contact the file's teeth. Overworking can flatten out the teeth, causing the snake to lose its scales.

1. Make sure you work this project at a yellow heat. Insert the roll bar into the hardy hole. Place the file end, teeth side down, against the roll bar (not shown) and the face of the anvil.

2. Using the cross peen of the hammer, strike down the center. This initiates the rolling process.

3. When enough of the file has been rolled, you can use just the anvil face and hit directly on the edge of the file to close the gap.

4. A roll bar hardy tool creates the space that anvils with chipping blocks have. Repetitive hits will curl the edges up, forming a channel. Work the metal while it is very hot and keep the curling as even as possible.

6. Once you have formed a nice taper on the tail end, you can continue the curl, moving up the remainder of the file.

5. Roll and close several inches of the file before turning it around and working the other end. You will need to switch tongs to accommodate the tubular shape.

7. If the seam starts to spiral, heat the area, secure it in the vise, and use your twisting wrench to untwist the section that is spiraling. This may have to be done several times while rolling the file lengthwise, but with practice, you will be able to perform this task without any distortions. Close the reminder of the file.

8. You are now ready to forge weld a plug into the head end of your snake. The purpose of this plug is to add mass into the snake head so that it can be forged into the appropriate shape.

Using tongs that can hold the tiny tapered point of the tail, heat the head and a tip of 3/8 inch (1 cm) -round stock that has been hot cut almost completely in half to a yellow forge welding temperature.

It is much easier and quicker to place the hot tip of the round stock into the snake head and twist it off from its parent stock than to have the little separate piece. The tip of the 3/8 inch (1 cm) will heat quicker, so when it's almost to welding temperature, dip the tip in your flux can and return it to the fire as the snake head reaches the yellow-white forging color temperature.

9. The trick to a successful first weld is to work quickly. So think about the moves while the pieces are heating up. Insert the tip into the file opening, twist off from the parent stock, and grab the hammer.

10. Work quickly and forge weld the plug into the opening. I've made rasp asps without the plug welded in, but I prefer the extra mass when it comes time to spread the jaws of the snake head out.

11. Shaping the snake head on a file is the same process as in the preceeding project. You should familiarize yourself with the forming by making smaller heads in round stock before attempting to make them from files.

12. The next step is to create the eyes of the snake. Secure the snake head into the vise with one side of its face out of the jaws. I made two chisels for the snake eyes. One is a circle for the eye and the second is a straight line, used to make a vertical pupil.

Use the circle chisel first and mark the pupil right in the middle. The jaws of the vise pull the heat out quickly, so have your chisels ready to stamp the eyes. Do not use the chisels on cold high carbon steel. It will damage the chisels' edges. Remember to quench the tips of the chisels after each use.

13. The snake in this project was made to be a porch door pull. Holes were punched in each end of the snake so that it could be mounted with screws or bolts.

14. Use your anvil and handheld bending forks to shape the snake.

Touchmark

A touchmark is your signature, stamped into the finished piece of ironwork. Included with your touchmark should be the year—the day and month are optional. A touchmark can be as simple as your initials, name, or business name stamped with a manufactured letter stamp set. My suggestion is to always use your name; your business name could change.

Touchmarks are a way of signing your work. There has been an active interest in creating a registry of touchmarks to ensure that the signatures will be traceable longer after we are not. By signing each piece you make with your own individual stamp, you give the work its seal of your authenticity.

My touchmark is simple—my initials L and S. I designed my touchmark to reflect my actual signature and the stamp has a rounded corner border to help make it stand out on my work.

Centaur Forge can help you create a custom touchmark, in lieu of using commercial stamps. If you opt for a custom stamp, I recommend that you order two of them—the second is cheaper because the artwork and die set has already been made.

Finishing Your Ironwork

GRINDING

Remember when you read about wrought iron's composition? It is so pure that oxidation does not occur. Mild steel has elements in it that will rust if the material is left untreated. Applying a finish to your iron is a necessity, whether the iron is for the interior or exterior of your home.

Before any kind of sealant or finish can be applied, all fire scale needs to be removed. If left on and coated over, with time and temperature changes it will pop off, exposing the bare metal. Most of the projects in this book are small enough that all preparatory clean up is minimal. When you start making those driveway gates and giant chandeliers, you will want to consider

Trick of the Trade

Sometimes scale sticks to the iron's surface, even after using a wire brush. For those pesky areas, I use an oxy-acetylene torch flame to release the scale. The iron should be at room temperature before you use the torch. It was explained to me that a quick change in temperature creates tension on the metal's surface, causing the scale to pop off.

the uses of sandblasting, powder coating, galvanizing, and chemical colorings as a means to seal and protect your work.

Regular brushing throughout the forging process will remove the majority of scale. If some remains on the surface, use a grinder with a knotted or twisted wire cup brush to finish the clean up process. These brushes can get into small areas and really make a piece shine. I prefer the twisted up brush to the plain cup brush because it is more aggressive and doesn't lose the wires as quickly.

All wire brushes on high-speed grinders lose their wires. There are better quality brushes on the market then others, but you do not necessarily need to buy the most expensive ones with the brand names. Either way, you need to wear both your safety glasses and a full-face shield. I have had wires fly out and hit the arm of another person 10 to 12 feet (3 to 3.7 m) away. If it hurts at that distance, imagine how it will feel up close. Wear long sleeves and tuck in your shirt. Loose clothing can easily get caught in the grinder. Leather aprons provide the best covering when using these brushes.

Whenever you use a grinder to clean your work, make sure the work is secured in a vise or clamped onto your work table. Even with those precautions, use of a high speed grinder will have its share of danger. Beware of kickback—the quick reverse action that occurs if the grinder rotation is interrupted.

OIL

Oil is the easiest sealant to use. You can use linseed oil, new or used motor oil, or food grade oil, which is necessary when treating iron objects that make contact with food.

The iron needs to be a certain temperature for the oil to soak into and seal. It is hotter than "to the touch," but not too hot that the oil will flame up once it is applied. If that happens, let the piece cool off a bit longer or quench it and start again. I call this temperature range rather warm. You should not be able to touch it with your bare hands.

WAX

Another method is to use a wax mixture that gets brushed on to rather warm metal and wiped off with a cloth. The wax mixture has equal parts of wax, turpentine, linseed oil, and a small amount of japan dryer. These four items are put into a pot, melted together, and then cooled. It will solidify enough to hold onto a brush for spreading, and if the iron is small enough, the piece can be dropped into the pot and quenched in wax. If you cannot find a source for bee's wax, use wax from a toilet bowl sealer. Be sure to buy wax without a flange. Hardware stores carry them.

PAINT

I do not like to hide my ironwork under paint of any color; there are rich, reflective surfaces that varnish when they are covered. I prefer wax varnish for outdoor pieces or a clear coat treatment, and powder coat in satin gray for large outdoor ironwork.

A brush can be used to apply a wax mixture to your ironwork.

—⁓—

What is success? Is it the ability to learn? Is it the ability to try? Is it the ability to be vulnerable and still come through? Is it the ability to say to yourself and others, "I burned myself making this BBQ fork!" If you have answered yes to all of these questions, then you are successful.

—⁓—

Conclusion

Taking the mystery out of blacksmithing does not take the magic out of the craft. When you understand how metal moves, and how to control the metal movement, you gain the knowledge, which enhances the magic.

Hopefully, you have learned the basics about moving metal. Once you have experienced the total process of the heat, the smells, the struggles, the power, and the creativity of blacksmithing, you will then be able to contribute and to enhance the magic.

RESOURCES

ORGANIZATIONS

ABANA
Artist Blacksmith Association of
   North America
www.abana.org
PO Box 816
Farmington, GA 30638
404.363.4009

BABA
British Artist Blacksmith Association
Rosebank, Plaxtol
Sevenoaks, Kent TN 15 OGL
England

CanIRON
Canadian Iron Association
www.geocities.com/caniron/index.html

NOMMA
National Ornamental and Miscellaneous
   Metals Association
www.nomma.org
1535 Pennsylvania Avenue
McDonough, GA 30253
888.516.8585

National Ornamental Museum
www.metalmuseum.org
374 Metal Museum Drive
Memphis, TN 38106
877.881.2326

SCHOOLS

Appalachian Center
   for the Crafts
1560 Craft Center Drive
Smithville, TN 37166
615.597.6801

Austin Community College
Riverside Campus
1020 Grove Boulevard
Austin, Texas 78741
512.223.6088

Brookfield Craft Center
PO Box 122, Route 25
Brookfield, CT 06804
203.775.4526

Cape Cod School of
   Blacksmithing
13 Captain Doane Way
Orleans, MA 02653

Cedar Lakes Craft Center
www.cedarlakes.com
HC 88 Box 21
Ripley, WV 25271
304.372.7873

The Center for Metal Arts
www.iceforge.com
PO Box 30
Chester, NY 10918
845.651.7550

Connecticut School of Wrought
   Iron Design
Box 8116
Buckland Station
Manchester, CT 06040
203.646.8363

Evanston Art Center
www.evanstonartcenter.org
2603 Sheridan Road
Evanston, IL 60201
847.475.5300

The Forgery School of Blacksmithing
13 Imnaha Road
Tijeras, NM 87059
505.281.8080

Guilford Art Center
www.guilfordartcenter.org
411 Church Street
Guilford, CT 06437
203.453.5947

Haystack Mountain School
   of Crafts
www.haystack-mtn.org
PO Box 518
Deer Isle, ME 04627
207.348.2306

John C. Campbell Folk School
www.folkschool.com
One Folk School Road
Brasstown, NC 28902
1.800.FOLK.SCH

McKenzie Career Center
7250 East 75th Street
Indianapolis, IN 46256
317.576.6420

New Brunswick Community College
1234 Mountain Road
Moncton, New Brunswick
E1C 8H9 Canada
506.856.2266

New England School of Metalwork
www.newenglandschoolofmetalwork.com
7 Albistan Way
Auburn, ME 04210
888.753-7502

Oregon College of Art & Craft
www.ocac.edu
8245 SW Barnes Road
Portland, OR 97225
503.297.5544

Ozark School of
   Blacksmithing, Inc.
www.ozarkschool.com
20183 West State HWY 8
Potosi, MO 63664
573.438.4725

Penland School of Crafts
www.penland.org
P.O. Box 37
Penland, NC 28765-0037
828.765.2359

Peters Valley Craft
   Education Center
www.pvcrafts.org
19 Kuhn Road
Layton, NJ 07851
973.948.5200

The Bill Pieh Resource
   for Metalwork
www.piehtool.com
Pieh Tool Company, Inc.
437 General Crook Trail, Suite D
Camp Verde, AZ 86322
888.743.4866

Rhode Island School of Design
www.risd.edu/ce.cfm
Extension Programs
2 College Street
Providence, RI 02903-2789
401.454.6200

Sir Sandford Fleming College
www.flemingc.on.ca
Box 839
Haliburton, Ontario, K0M 1S0
Canada
705.457.1680

**Southern Illinois University
   at Carbondale**
www.siuc.edu
PO Box 4301
Carbondale, IL 62901-4301
618.453.4315
offers an MS in Blacksmithing

Texarkana College
www.tc.cc.tx.us
2500 N. Robison Road
Texarkana, TX 75599
903.838.4541 Ext 3236

**Turley Forge
   Blacksmithing School**
www.turleyforge.com
919-A Chicoma Vista
Santa Fe, NM 87507
505.471.8608

**University of North Carolina,
   Charlotte**
www.uncc.edu
Hwy 49
Charlotte, NC 28223
704.547.3361

University of Washington
www.art.washington.edu
Metals Program
School of Art Box 353440
Seattle, WA 98195
206.543.0970

Warwickshire College
www.warkscol.ac.uk
Moreton Morrell
Warwick, CV35 9BL
England
011.44.01926.318318

West Dean College
www.westdean.org.uk
West Dean, Chichester
West Sussex, P018 OQZ
England

Worcester Center for Crafts
25 Sagamore Rd
Worcester, MA 01605
508.753.8183

MAGAZINES AND PUBLICATIONS

Anvil Magazine
www.anvilmag.com

The Anvil's Ring
ABANA Publication
thering@sebastianpublishing.com

Blacksmith's Gazette
www.fholder.com
950 South Falcon Road
Camano Island, WA 98292

Blacksmith's Journal
www.blacksmithsjournal.com
Hoffmann Publications, Inc.
PO Box 1699
Washington, MO 63090
800.944.6134

Hammer's Blow
ABANA Publication
hammerguy@mindspring.com
3404 Hartford Drive
Chattanooga, TN 37415

Hephaistos
   German publication with
   English translation available
www.metall-aktiv.de/

WEBSITES

The American Bladesmith Society
www.americanbladesmith.com
The art and science of forging knives

Anvil Fire
www.anvilfire.com
*Includes forums, gallery, book reviews,
   plans, news, and how-to*

The ArtMetal Project
www.artmetal.com/project
*An educational resource for the
   metal arts*

www.blacksmithchic.com
Welcome to my vortex of hot metal

www.thefabricator.com
Metal fabricating resource

The Forge and Anvil Online
www.gactr.uga.edu/tv/forge/
The Georgia Center for Continuing
   Education Site
Blacksmithing and metalwork

Iron News
www.ironnews.com
The world of wrought iron

SUPPLIERS

Atlantic Steel Corp. - tool steel
35-27 36th Street
Astoria, NY 11106
212.729.4800

Breakthrough
Vanex Inc.
800.851.7390
*Excellent industrial grade acrylic finish—
I recommend Clear Satin 50-0.*

Centaur Forge Ltd.
117 North Spring Street
Burlington, WI 53105
414.763.9175
*Supplies and custom touchmark
   services*

Crescent City Iron Supply
www.crescentcityironsupply.com
Westchester, IL
Kenner, LA
800.535.9842
Ornamental iron components

King Architectural Metals
www.kingmetals.com
800.542.2379
Ornamental iron components

Laser Precision Cutting
joevog@aol.com
117 David Biddle Trail
Weaverville, NC 28787
800.635.2596

Lawler Foundry Corporation
PO Box 320069
Birmingham, AL 35232
1.800.624.9512
Castings and forgings

Frank Morrow Company
Decorative Metal Stamping
129 Baker Street
Providence, RI 02905
800.556.7688

Patina Solutions
800.822.7004

Tennessee Fabricating Company
2025 York Avenue
Memphis, TN 38104
800.258.4766
Cast iron components

Triple S Chemical Products
1413 Mirasol Street
Los Angeles, CA 90023
213.385.3401
Patina

Working Metal
Dean Rose
409 East Springfield Avenue
Champaign, IL 61820
217.355.6510
Offers casting services

EQUIPMENT

A Cut Above
800.444.2999
*Cutting, grinding, and finishing
  products*

**Bob Bergman – Postville
  Power Hammer**
N8126 Postville Road
Blanchardville, WI 53516
608.527.2494

Big Blu Blacksmith Air Hammer
www.bigbluhammer.com

Bullhammer Technology
www.bullhammer.com
US: 2000 Riverside Drive
Asheville, NC 28804
877.843.2855

UK: 2 Gordon Road
Waltham Abbey, Essex EN9 1DR
England
044.(0)836.340171
*Pneumatic forging hammers, forges,
  air compressors*

Euroanvils
www.euroanvils.net
PO Box 3766
Chester, VA 23831
804.530.0290
Traditional European anvils

Forge and Anvil Metal Studio
www.forgeandanvil.com
30 King Street
St. Jacobs, Ontario N0B 2N0
Canada
519.664.3622
Anvils

Grainger
www.grainger.com
800.473.3473
Tools and supplies

Ironwood, LLC
www.powerhammers.com
10385 Long Road
Arlington, TN 38002
901.867.7300
Air hammers and dies

John Crouchet
www.texaswroughtiron.com
*He can and will tell you all that you
  need to know about fly presses.*

**Kayne and Son Custom
  Hardware, Inc.**
www.kayneandson.com
www.blacksmithdepot.com
100 Daniel Ridge Road
Candler, NC 28715
828.667.8868

Koka Metalsmiths
www.kokametalsmiths.com
PO Box 237
Dakota, MN 55925
507.643.7946
Hand forged hammers and chasing tools

Little Giant/Mayer Bros.
420 Fourth Corso
Nebraska City, NE 68410
402.873.6603
Power hammer parts and service

McMaster-Carr
www.mcmaster.com
P.O. Box 4355
Chicago, IL 60680-4355
630.833.0300
General tool and equipment supplier

NC Tool Company Inc
www.nctool.com
6133 Hunt Road
Pleasant Garden, NC 27313
800.446.6498

Nimba Anvils
www.anvils.nimbaforge.com
353 Glen Cove Road
Port Townsend, WA 98368
360.385.7258

Pieh Tool Company Inc.
www.piehtoolco.com
437 W. Hwy 260 Suite D
Camp Verde, AZ 86322
928.554.070

Sparky Abrasives
zsparky@aol.com
Minneapolis, MN 55429
800.328.4560

Striker Tool Company
www.strikertools.com
3939 W. Capitol Avenue, Suite E
West Sacramento, CA 95691
866.290.1263

GLOSSARY

Alloy—mixture of two or more metals, usually fused, but combined in a molten state.

Annealing—a heating process used to soften metal.

Anvil—a heavy, steel-faced iron block on which metal is hammered.

Anvil Tools—also called hardy tools or bottom tools. Tools with square shanks that are inserted to the hardy hole of the anvil.

Bank—to cover a forge fire with green coal and adjust the air flow to keep the fire lit but in an inactive state.

Bevel—the angle that one surface or line makes with another when they are not at right angles.

Bick—the horn or pointed end of the anvil.

Bituminous—bituminous coal is an organic sedimentary rock formed by the compression of peat bog material. This black, sometimes dark brown, soft coal burns easily and produces smoky yellow flames.

Burnish—to add a gloss or luster to a material by rubbing; to add the color of a soft metal to iron by brushing it on.

Center punch—a short punch with a sharp pointed end that is used to mark metal for tasks such as drilling or punching.

Chase—to make indentations into metal.

Chisel—a metal tool with a sharpened edge.

Clinker—gummy, solidified wastes comprising the impurities that accumulate as you continue to burn coal.

Coke—to add water to a coal fire to produce coke. Also a term used for purified coal, or the porous residue that forms after the sulfur and other impurities have burned out of the coal.

Cold cut—a handled or anvil tool used to cut cold metal. Its cutting edge is blunter and shorter than a hot cut.

Collar—a piece of metal wrapped around two or more pieces of ironwork to hold them together.

Countersink—a hole with beveled side. It is used to set the head of a rivet at or below the surface.

Cupping tool—a tool with a rounded depression used to create a finished dome-end on a rivet. Also called a Rivet Set.

Curie Point or Curie—the temperature at which ferromagnetic materials, such as iron and iron alloys, lose their ability to be magnetized.

Die—a pair of cutting or shaping tools that when moved toward each other produce a desired form or impression.

Divider—a measuring or marking instrument with two adjustable arms.

Draw down—to make a piece of metal thinner, smaller, and longer.

Drift—a shaping and refining tool driven through a punched hole.

Fire scale—the oxidation that occurs when metal is heated.

Flush—on a level with adjacent surfaces.

Flux—a substance used to promote the fusion of metal by cleaning and removing oxidation. It is applied to two metal surfaces before forge welding.

Forge—a furnace where metal is heated or a shop with a furnace where metal is heated and hammered.

Forge welding—the process of joining two or more pieces of iron or steel by heating the material surfaces until they are almost molten and then hammering the pieces together.

Fuller—a metal tool with a blunt convex end that is used to indent or spread heated metal.

Green coal—unburned fresh coal.

Hardening—this process is usually associated with toolmaking. Heat treating steel to harden it.

Hardy hole—this is the square hole located on the face of the anvil that is used to secure anvil or hardy tools.

Heat—duration of time a piece of metal is hot enough to be forged.

Heat treat—to treat metal by heating and cooling in a way to promote desired qualities in the stock material.

Hold down or hold fast—an anvil tool used to secure metal stock in the pritchel hole to the anvil face.

Hot cut—an anvil tool used to cut hot metal. It has a sharper edge than a cold cut.

Jaw—two or more opposing parts that open and close to hold or crush materials.

Jig—a tool used as a guide for forming metal. Especially convenient when mass producing a particular shape.

Mandrel—a round bar over which iron is shaped and formed.

Monkey tool—A tool that is used to finish hand-forged tenons. It refines the shape of the tenon while also squaring its shoulders.

Mortise—a hole cut into or through one piece to receive another piece.

Oxy-acetylene—a fuel that is generated by the burning of acetylene in the presence of oxygen.

Parent stock—the primary or largest piece of stock used in an exercise or project.

Peen—the domed or wedge-shaped end of a hammer, located opposite the face, that is used to bend and shape metal.

Planish—to smooth, toughen, and finish metal by hammering lightly.

Pritchel hole—the round shape hole located on the face of the anvil.

Pritchel plate—a tool used when punching holes that is made from plate steel and it has a variety of differently sized holes.

Punch—a pointed tool used to make marks and holes.

Quench—to cool heated metal by immersing it in water or oil.

Reins—the handles on a set of tongs.

Rheostat—an instrument which regulates the passage of electric current.

Riveting—The process of mechanically joining two or more pieces of material. A bolt with a head on one end is inserted through aligned holes in the materials and then the plain end of the rivet is hammered to form a head which secures the materials together.

Rivet Set—a tool with a rounded depression used to create a finished dome-end on a rivet. Also called a Cupping Tool.

Rodded—a hand tool that is wrapped with steel to create a handle.

Scarf—to create two angled surfaces on two pieces of metal in preparation for forge welding.

Scriber—a sharp pointed tool used to mark metal.

Scroll—a spiral.

Slag—the refuse created when metal is heated and hammered.

Sledge—a large heavy hammer that usually requires a two-handed grip to swing.

Slit Chisel—a marking or cutting tool usually made of tempered steel consisting of a sharpened edge attached to a straight handle.

Smelt—the process of melting ores to separate the metallic elements. Iron and steel are smelted from iron ore.

Smith—someone who works with metals.

Smithy—a blacksmith or the shop of.

Spring set—a pair of top and bottom tools connected by a spring. If a hardy shank is attached, it is called a hardy spring set.

Stock—the steel materials used in blacksmithing.

Striker—a blacksmith's helper who swings the sledgehammer.

Swage—a concave tool used to shape metal.

Swage block—a cast iron block with shaped holes and swage grooves that is used to shape metal.

Taper—forging a gradual reduction in metal.

Tempering—to bring to the desired degree of hardness, usually by heat-treating and cooling.

Tenon—an end of a piece of metal specially shaped with a shoulder, to fit into a mortise or a hole.

Tongs—a tool used to pick up metal commonly consisting of two pieces joined at a pivot.

Tool steel—a carbon or alloy steel that is appropriate for making tools, with a carbon content ranging between 0.7 and 1.4 percent. Its hardness and strength allows tools to maintain a cutting edge, even under elevated temperatures.

Trip hammer—a mechanical hammer that is operated by a foot control.

Twist—to form metal into a spiral shape.

Upsetting—compacting metal to make it shorter and/or thicker.

Vise—a tool with two jaws that close by screw, used to hold material.

Weld—the fusion of metals when heat is applied.

Working triangle—the area in a blacksmith shop located between the forge, anvil, and vise.

Wrapping—winding a heated piece of stock around two or more other pieces of stock and creating a joint.

INDEX

Acknowledgments

When there are so many people who have contributed to my life and where I am at right now, well, that would be another chapter in this book. Therefore, I would like to say thank you to my teachers, my family and friends, and everyone who has supported my art and business.

My utmost gratitude goes to Queue McMillan. My mother Christine Zack and father William Sims, whose support, even when I said I wanted to make my living as a blacksmith, did not waiver. Jobie Spencer, the man who felt sorry for me when I just started out then proceeded to help me acquire the majority of my tools and equipment. Daniel Broten, my good friend and the photographer of this book. Elmer Roush, the man who agreed to take me on as an apprentice, all those years ago. Special thanks to Scott Swanson, my first forging partner, and Robert Owings, whose experience in book writing and proofreading saved my butt. My friends and colleagues in the blacksmithing community, thwarted or not, thank you for being there. The town of Charleston, Illinois. I love my hometown and I am proud to be here. The local businesses who have always assisted me and my business, namely Charleston Glass Company, Eastern Electric Supply Company, Gano Welding and Supply, McFarland Steel, and General Steel—my home away from home. The publishers, especially Delilah, Rosalind, Winnie, Betsy, Liz, Mary, and Candice—thank you for finding me.

And finally, a big thank you to you, the reader of this book. You are embarking on a wonderful adventure with this powerful craft.

Photo by Lawrence McGowan

About the Author

Lorelei Sims is a self-employed artist-blacksmith who opened her studio, Five Points Blacksmith Shop, in 1993. She incorporates traditional blacksmithing techniques with the use of modern equipment. Her commissions are quite varied, with a major portion of these directed toward a functional use in the home and garden. With recent public art commissions dedicated to indigenous plants of the Midwest, Lorelei has had the opportunity to continue her research and development of forging and fabricating botanical forms in iron.

A typical day in her smithy may include repairs on old cast iron, antique iron restoration, fabricating and welding vehicles and trailers, as well as on-site welding repair to fix everything from railings to railroad cars.

Her growth as an artist is fueled by the knowledge that her work is enjoyed by many and that her business is valued by her community. Lorelei's hobbies outside of visiting the scrap yard include gardening, cooking, hostessing, traveling, demonstrating, and procrastinating.

To view Lorelei's artwork, visit her website, www.blacksmithchic.com.